NATURAL HITTER'S

Drill Handbook

THE

Vol. 1

101

BASIC HITTING DRILLS

Luis Ortiz

COACHES
CHOICE™

ISBN: 1-58518-950-2
Library of Congress Control Number: 2005937284
Cover design: Jeanne Hamilton
Book layout: Jeanne Hamilton
Front cover photo: Ezra Shaw/Getty Images

Coaches Choice
P.O. Box 1828
Monterey, CA 93942
www.coacheschoice.com

Dedication

I want to dedicate this book:

- To my daughters, Gabriela, Naomi, Samantha (Boo-boo), and Moriah (Bebe), and my wife, Susan, for their patience and love.
- To my mother, Isabel, my dad, Luis, my brother, Yiyo, and my sisters, Tania and Ana, for their love, support, and encouragement in all the endeavors of my life.
- To Miguelo for pitching to me all those corn seeds and for holding the tire for me to hit it.
- To my dear friend Jason Ledbetter for being a brother to me, an uncle to my daughters, and a friend that I can always count on.
- To all those kids that I have worked with through the winters who unknowingly tested many of these drills and provided the information I needed to write this book.

Acknowledgments

First, I would like to thank God for his love and mercy.

I want to thank all of my friends (coaches and players) that provided insight with the drills they have used to become better hitters.

Finally, I would like to thank Gabriela Ortiz for all the hard work she did in the preparation of this book.

Preface

My personal philosophy is that kids learn faster and better when they are having fun. The hitting lessons I teach and the instructional camps I help conduct are full of information, but that information is usually intertwined with analogies and drills that make hitting fun.

Even though I was not aware of the value of incorporating fun into my teaching efforts at the time, I started writing this book a long time ago. During my baseball journey, I have been blessed with playing in different countries and with players from all over the world. Since as long as I can remember, I have been writing down every hitting drill that I have seen or heard about, from the sophisticated drills used in Japan to the "take-advantage-of-everything approach" employed in the Dominican Republic and Cuba. I would always ask my friends what drills they usually did to get better. I then started creating drills for my own personal use or to help a teammate or client. This book is my initial venture into the writing world, even though *The Natural Hitter's Handbook* was actually published first. I started writing it all the way back in the mid-90s, when I was struggling a lot with injuries and wanted to prepare myself for life after baseball. I cannot believe how many drills I have gathered—so many, in fact, that I had to divide them into multiple volumes. I hope that you can find a number of drills in these volumes that help your players become the best hitters they can be. Have them follow the instructions for each drill, but do not be afraid of improvising for each player's personal hitting needs. All you can ask your hitters to do is to work hard, have fun, and persevere. Talk to each player, and have him watch himself on video to diagnose whatever problems he may be experiencing and then identify drills that target them. Look for drills that are appropriate for each individual, taking into consideration the equipment available, the weather, if he will be doing them alone or with a partner, and any other circumstances that are unique to that particular player.

This book includes 101 basic hitting drills; some might work for a particular player, while others might not. Hitting is a very personal matter, and no magic formula exists that will make a hitter better. But with trial and error, each hitter can learn what works for him.

Throughout my career, I have always been interested in hitting drills. Very few hitters can listen to what their coaches are saying (explaining what they want them to do) and apply the relevant points immediately to their swing. On the contrary, most players are "practical doers." They develop a feel for what their coaches are saying by actually doing it, not by simply listening. They develop muscle memory by repeating a drill that targets the mechanics the coach wants them to master or a bad habit they may be trying to break.

I have always been interested in hitting drills for other reasons as well. For one thing, it seems that at one time or another I have had every bad hitting habit that you can think of, and for another, I was always trying to find a better way to compete against teammates and opponents, particularly those who may have been using performance-enhancement drugs. I wanted to get the best out of my natural ability, not by cheating and using drugs, but by working hard and being smart. As a result, I have always been on the lookout for a practice drill that might help improve my swing. This drill book series is a compilation of all the drills that I learned through the years or that I developed myself either for my own personal hitting improvement or to help a teammate or client during the off-season.

Contents

1

Overview

The Six Basic Drills

Before players begin utilizing hitting drills to improve their technique, you must teach them the six basic drills: dry swings, tee work, soft toss, flips, batting practice, and batting machine. These basics are the foundation for every drill included in this book, so it is essential that your players master them before moving on to more difficult drills.

One goal of this book was to keep things simple by using tips and pictures to help along the way. The following are terms used to keep things clear within each drill:

- Objectives—how the drill can help improve hitting technique
- Degree of Difficulty

    1B: Easy

    2B: Medium

    3B: Difficult

    HR: Extremely difficult

    GS: Most difficult
- Equipment Needed
- Description—step-by-step information on how to perform the drill
- Coaching Points—additional information, reminders, and safety guidelines to help your players get the most benefit from the drill

Dry Swings

A dry swing—a 1B-level tool—is a swing taken when there is not a ball involved. In other words, all you need for drills involving dry swings is a bat and some open space. Despite the simplicity, dry swings can be effective in teaching hitting mechanics, warming up for practice or games, and improving bat speed (when performed with different bat sizes).

To develop proper hitting mechanics, the hitter dry swings as follows:

- Stride: The front foot should be soft on the landing and point to home plate. The hands are taken back.

Dry swings

- The hitter takes his chin shoulder to shoulder during the swing.
- The back foot is pivoted as if squishing a bug.
- The hitter keeps his head down, eyes on contact (visualize).
- Nice, short, and quick swing full of balance. The hitter swings down.
- For improving bat speed, the hitter swings his bat as fast as he can until he is fatigued.

Because dry swings do not feature a ball, the hitter can concentrate on his mechanics. He does not need to rush the swing as if a ball is involved.

Tee Work

Tee work can be used to correct and master hitting mechanics and as a way to discipline a hitter to stay back better so he can keep his power on his backside and improve his balance. Tee work will also help the hitter develop proper muscle memory. Tee work—a 2B-level tool—allows a hitter to focus on proper hitting mechanics and make adjustments. The equipment needed in tee work drills is a tee, baseballs, a bat, and a batting cage or hitting net.

To perform these drills, the hitter needs to take his stride, land in his launching position, and "freeze." The hitter then swings the bat, aiming to hit the inside of the ball, or the seam closer to him (the ball should be

Tee work

Soft tosses

set on the tee so the seams run perpendicular to the ground). During the swing, the hitter needs to go right to the ball, keeping his arms close to the body and letting the hands work first instead of the legs (the back knee follows the hands).

As a coach, it is important to emphasize a strong launching position and a proper hitting box, with the elbows pointing down, the front leg firm, the back knee flexed, and the back foot planted on the ground. The strength of this position dictates how the hitter hits the ball.

Soft Tosses

Soft tosses—another 2B-level tool—allow a hitter to take a lot of swings at a moving target without getting too tired, while also improving mechanics and bat speed. Soft tosses require a partner (or a "feeder") to toss the pitches, in addition to baseballs, a bat, a batting cage, and possibly a screen to protect the feeder.

To perform soft tosses, the hitter takes his normal stance at home plate as a partner positions himself on the other side of the plate in a 45-degree angle to the hitter. The partner is either on one of his knees or sits on a chair. The distance between hitter and feeder is about eight to 10 feet, a distance at which the feeder

will not get hit by the bat. When the hitter and the feeder are in the right position, the feeder then softly tosses the ball underhand to the hitter. The hitter waits back and hits the ball right to the middle of the net. The hitter will have to experiment with where he wants the ball to be tossed and occasionally may want to vary the location of the toss.

This drill is one of the best available for developing sound mechanics and improving bat speed, and is performed almost every day by professional players before practices and games.

Flips

Flips are similar to soft tosses in that they improve a hitter's mechanics while saving the thrower's arm. A 2B-level tool, flips require a bat, baseballs, a batting cage or field, a screen, and maybe a chair. The hitter should do this drill often. Most professional hitters take flips before every batting practice.

The person flipping the balls gets behind the screen about 15 to 20 feet in front of the hitter, in the direction where a pitcher would set up. The "flipper" tosses the ball underhand in a softball motion. He tosses the ball over the plate as the hitter aims to hit the screen every time, always focusing on good mechanics. Remind the flipper to make sure he brings

Flips

Batting practice

his arm behind the screen quickly after releasing the ball to avoid being hit. It is easier for the flipper to do this when standing up, but it can be done sitting down as well.

Timing is of the essence in this drill. The hitter starts the swing process (striding) when the flipper is taking his arm back. The hitter should be landing the front foot just as the flipper is letting go of the ball to ensure a separation of the stride and hands.

Batting Practice

Batting practice mimics game conditions, thereby improving the hitter's timing and preparing him for game speed. This drill allows the hitter to see how hard and to where he is hitting the ball. Batting practice—a 2B-level tool—requires baseballs, a bat, helmet, partner, and either a batting cage or a field and "L" screen.

The hitter sets up at home plate with the partner about two-thirds of the way to the pitcher's mound. The partner then tosses the ball by mimicking a pitcher's windup and throwing fastballs straight and firm (though not too hard). At the hitter's request the partner can throw off-speed pitches. Batting practices are usually done in groups of three to five hitters, and usually with five rounds per group.

Every hitter needs to use batting practice to get better and get ready for the game, not as a home run hitting contest. The hitter should practice his game plan and prepare to do what he might do in the game.

Professional baseball teams often follow a batting practice routine that goes something like this:

Round 1: Two bunts, one hit and run, one move the runner, five hits to the opposite field

Round 2: One infield in, one infield back, five hits, one squeeze bunt

Round 3: Five hits (hit it where it is pitched)

Round 4: Three hits (driving the ball)

Round 5: Base hit rounds (if the hitter gets a hit, he keeps hitting; if he gets an out, the next hitter hits). If there is time, another base hit round is done.

Batting Machine

Batting machine practice drills allow hitters to practice their swings often and to see different speeds during the drill. A 2B-level tool, batting machine drills require a bat, baseballs, a batting machine, and a batting cage.

A hitter swinging off a batting machine needs to move around home plate to simulate inside, outside, low, high, hard, and slow pitches. The hitter should always wear a helmet to protect himself.

Batting machine

To develop a great swing, a combination of these types of drills should be performed every day. For example, professional hitters, the best in the business, do underhand flips, tee work, and batting practice before nearly every game. They might do them with their own personal touch to target a problem or a feel, but they consistently do these drills because they know that they keep them sharp or help them get out of slumps when they are struggling.

Every player needs to develop his own program, with drills that keep his swing consistent and razor-sharp. When setting up this program, the coach can combine two or three drills of different types to accelerate a player's improvement. For example, perform soft toss hitting colored balls with a heavy bat. Soft toss helps improve hitting mechanics, while colored balls improve how well a hitter sees the ball. And with the heavy bat, the player will be overloading his hitting muscles and getting stronger. You will save time by having each player perform hard, smart work.

Off-season vs. In-season

During the off-season, each player should perform drills that make him stronger, help him swing faster, and make his swing mechanically sound. Off-season drill work is especially important for players whose regular seasons involve a lot of games each week.

Players who only play one or two games a week can continue doing the same drills that they were doing during the off-season, but should avoid overload and/or overspeed drills before a game. Mechanics drills can and should be done every single day of the season, but be sure to work on quality over quantity.

Players who play four to seven days a week should perform in-season drills that reinforce what they did during the off-season and back off of the overload/overspeed drills so they do not fatigue during the game or run out of gas during the second half of the season. This guideline does not apply to backup players who are not playing much. These hitters should take advantage of their time, push themselves, and make themselves better by working harder so they can eventually become regulars.

Remember, every player is different. Some hitters love to work hard every day and it does not seem to affect their game, while others cannot do it. Learn about each player. Have them make mental notes of how they feel during games after different levels of intensity during practice and then find a level that keeps them energized during the whole game. Also, remind your team that getting good sleep and having a nutritious diet will also help them stay stronger longer.

Every player must work hard to find the routine that works best for him. Once it is found, help the player to be consistent with it so he stays in top condition during the whole year. It is better to do a little work every day than a lot once in a while.

Proper Drill Workout Sequence

Players should use the following sequence when doing drills:

- Warm-up
- Bat speed, power, and reaction drills
- Mechanics and mental drills (improve skills)
- Balance, hand-eye coordination, and vision drills
- Team and game situation drills
- Overload drills

- Conditioning drills
- Cool-down

For example, if on Monday the team is doing bat speed and vision drills the sequence should be warm-up, bat speed drills, vision drills, and cool-down. Bat speed, power, and reaction drills should be done first because players should be as fresh as possible when trying to improve power and bat speed. Conditioning drills come last because the goal is to improve work capacity and will power (the ability to keep going when wanting to quit) and these are best improved when players are already tired.

The following guidelines will help the team get the most out of drills. Distribute this list to every player.

- Concentrate and think about what you are doing. A drill is supposed to feel mechanical at first, but the more you do it, the more natural it will become.
- Do drills game speed. Do not simply go through the motions. You need to mimic game conditions even if you are doing tee work or dry swinging. Do the drills in the manner you want to perform during the game. You might feel slow at the beginning, but always perform drills with intensity.
- Be safe. Before doing a drill, look around so you do not hit anybody. Tell people what you are doing if they are on the field. Use tennis shoes in the cage or on a carpet. Do not overstrain yourself. If it hurts, stop. Use batting gloves to prevent blisters whenever you are taking a lot of swings.
- Do not overdo it. Stop when you are getting tired or when the intensity level is decreasing. When you are tired, you will either begin using the very habit you are working to break or help yourself with other parts of the body, thereby creating additional problems.
- With drills that require a partner, make sure that the feeder knows what he is doing and what you are trying to accomplish. He needs to be accurate and be able to point out when you are doing something right or wrong. He needs to make sure that he stays behind the screen at all times.
- Grow into each drill. If you are a beginner, stick with the beginner's drills and move up as you get

better and stronger. Do not get ahead of yourself. It is more beneficial to do something right at an easier level than to be inconsistent at a more difficult one.
- Do what the drill tells you to do, but do not be afraid to change it to your advantage. It is your drill now, so target your personal need even if that requires adjusting the drill.
- Ask your coach what you need to work on, and then find a drill that targets your needs.
- Always do a set of regular swings after doing the drill so you can transfer the feeling of the drill to your swing.
- To improve bat speed and power swing faster than you normally do. Challenge yourself to do more than you think possible.
- The keys of success are:
  - ✓ Be intense—work hard, pay the price.
  - ✓ Be persistent—work often, be patient (the race is not always won by the strongest or fastest, but by the one that lasts the longest). Remember, the key of succeeding with a drill is repetition.
  - ✓ Be smart—work with a plan, do what works for you.
  - ✓ Enjoy what you are doing.

Begin the drill-selection process by looking at what problem a drill targets, what skill level it requires, and whether you have the equipment to do it in practice. After you have checked the drills and found the ones that target a particular player's problem, be persistent and have the player perform the drill often. Repetition is the key for any muscle memory practice. Remember, you are helping the players to get rid of something (i.e., a bad habit) they have been doing for a while, so give them the time needed to eliminate the problem and succeed. Remind the players that they need to repeat a good habit for a few weeks if they want to get rid of an old bad habit. They must be patient, work hard, and be smart. If they do that they will conquer any hitting problem they might have and become the hitters they believe they can be.

2

Drills to Mentally Prepare to Hit the Ball Hard

Drill #1: 1, 2, 3, 4 Breathing Drill

Objectives:
- Emphasizes proper breathing throughout the swing
- Teaches the hitter rhythm during the stance
- Helps the hitter release tension for a quicker swing

Degree of Difficulty:
- Dry swing: 1B
- Tee work: 1B
- Soft toss: 2B
- Flips: 2B
- Batting practice: 3B

Equipment Needed:
- Bat
- Baseballs
- Batting cage, hitting net, baseball field, or open space
- Partner
- Optional: Tee

Description: Many coaches can spot a hitter who looks tight or tense during the swing, but most of them do not know how to help that hitter look and feel relaxed. A hitter looks tense during the swing when he is holding his breath as he goes through the hitting process. When a hitter holds his breath, he not only appears tight, but the swing is harder to execute as well. Teach the hitter to blow the air out of his lungs as he swings. To execute this drill, the hitter:

- Mimics a swing forward to the pitcher and exhales.
- Swings back to the catcher (as if he is rewinding his swing) and inhales.
- Swings forward again and exhales again.
- Takes his stride while slowly breathing in and gathering strength before he starts his swing. He then holds his breath during the launching position. When he starts his swing, he explosively exhales as if blowing his hands away from him to hit the ball.

Coaching Points:
- The slower the inhalation during the stride, the softer the approach to the ball.
- The first few times a hitter performs this drill, breathing deeply might make the hitter feel a little lightheaded. The hitter should not get discouraged and should just keep working on it.
- Breathing is a good timing mechanism if the hitter decides to incorporate this approach to his regular hitting process.

Drill #2: Analogy Visualization

Objectives:
- Teaches young hitters how to utilize different hitting mechanics
- Gives hitters something concrete to think about when practicing a specific mechanic

Degree of Difficulty: 1B

Equipment Needed:
- Bat
- Baseballs
- Batting cage or baseball field

Description: This drill will give the hitter a visual idea of what to do when he is learning a new hitting mechanic. Following are some of the visualizations a coach can use with young hitters:

- The bat is a torch and the top end of the bat is on fire. This visualization helps put the bat in a good position to hit (i.e., not letting the bat collapse) and keep the bat away from the body for hitters who wrap. When you see that the bat is collapsing, tell the hitter that he is going to get burned or is getting hot, hot, hot.
- Each elbow is an eye and those eyes are looking at the ground. Use this analogy with hitters who raise their elbows to put the hitter in a good position to hit (i.e., in a hitting box during the stance).

The following analogies can be used to help the hitter land the foot softly on the ground:

- A baby is sleeping and the hitter must be careful not to wake her up by stepping too hard with the front foot.
- The front shoe is made of glass and if the hitter steps too hard it is going to break.
- The front foot is landing on thin ice and if the hitter lands too hard he will fall into the freezing water.
- An invisible rubber band connects the front foot to the hands. The hitter stretches the cord to separate his hands from the stride and take the hands back properly (Figure A).

Figure A

Figure B

- The same rubber band visualized in the previous analogy can be visualized as a slingshot to have the hitter take the bat head right to the ball and swing with power, making him believe that the stretched cord is shooting the hands toward the ball. (Figure B).
- An invisible rope is connecting the end of the bat to the ceiling (in a 45-degree angle). The idea is for the hitter to pull the rope from the ceiling, making a hole in the ceiling. This will teach the hitter to take the bat head right to the ball (Figure C).
- Batman, Robin, and the Joker. The front shoulder is Batman, the back shoulder is Robin, and the chin is the Joker. Batman catches the Joker as the hitter is taking the hands back, the Joker gets away at the beginning of the swing, but Robin catches him to finish the swing. This analogy teaches the hitter to swing by taking his chin from shoulder to shoulder.
- The hitter visualizes a bug under his big toe and then pivots his back foot, squishing the bug. This will teach the hitter to rotate properly.
- The hitter visualizes himself as a samurai and his bat is his sword. He tries to cut the ball in half with his bat. This analogy teaches the hitter to swing through the ball.

- The hitter pushes the ball away from himself, thereby learning to swing through the ball.
- The hitter finishes his swing and holds that position for a few seconds resembling a statue. This analogy helps the hitter develop balance at the end of the swing.
- The hitter visualizes that he is taking the picture for his baseball card. This analogy is also used to develop balance at the end of the swing. The hitter swings and freezes at the end of the follow-through to pose for mom or dad to take a picture. If he shakes (loses his balance), the picture will be blurry.

Coaching Points:
- These visualizations work especially well with young hitters.
- Always use your imagination when teaching younger hitters. Most hitters would not really understand what swinging down means, but most of them would do it well if you tell them to throw the knob of the bat down to the front foot.

Figure C

Drill #3: Rhythm—Pendulum/Level Swing/Bat Circle

Objectives:
• Teaches the hitter to have rhythm during the stance
• Relaxes the hitter, allowing him to swing faster

Degree of Difficulty: 1B

Equipment Needed:
• Bat
• Batting cage, open space, or baseball field

Description: The following movements are used during the stance to keep the hitter relaxed, flexible, and ready to start the swing process. These movements can also be used during the at bat when the pitcher is taking the signs from the catcher.
• The pendulum: The hitter moves the bat back and forth like a pendulum as the pitcher is taking the signs from the catcher. He then takes his bat up and remains still during the delivery.

• The level swing: The hitter mimics a level swing as he is waiting for the pitcher to throw the ball. The hitter does not follow through; instead, he swings until contact to where the hands are in a "palm up, palm down" position and then brings the bat back to the launching position.
• The bat circle: The hitter sets up in his stance and moves the hands in a counterclockwise motion making a small circle with the top of the bat head.

Coaching Points:
• The hitter can add breathing to the movement. For example, when the hitter takes the bat to the pitcher he breathes out and when he brings the bat back he breathes in. He does the same thing during the swing—breathes in when he is gathering power and breathes out as he starts the swing (blowing his hands away from him).
• The hitter needs to relax not only his body but also his mind. He needs to keep his mind clear to make any necessary adjustment during the at bat.

Drill #4: Imitate Your Favorite Hitter

Objectives:
- Gives the hitter instant confidence
- Improves the hitter's swing by giving him a better hitter's swing to emulate

Degree of Difficulty: 2B

Equipment Needed:
- Bat
- Baseballs
- Batting cage, baseball field, or hitting net
- Partner

Description: The hitter tries to imitate how his favorite hitter swings, as well as how he behaves when he is hitting a baseball—how confident he is, how relaxed he is, etc. This is a good drill for talented hitters who doubt their abilities.

Coaching Point:
- Performing this drill does not give the hitter permission to change his approach. It simply provides a way to free a hitter from some of his doubts so he will start swinging more naturally.

Otto Greule Jr/Getty Images

Drill #5: Hitting to All Fields

Objectives:
• Improves bat control
• Teaches the hitter how to hit to all fields

Degree of Difficulty: 2B

Equipment Needed:
• Bat
• Baseballs
• Partner
• Baseball field

Description: This drill can be done during batting practice and the hitters in each group can compete against each other. Each hitter gets 10 pitches and tries to hit them as follows:
• First three balls the opposite way
• Next four balls right up the middle
• Last three balls to the pull side
• The other hitters in the group judge the hitter, giving him one point for each successful attempt.

Coaching Point:
• The hitter is almost in hit-and-run mode in that he is swinging at each pitch, making sure he is trying to hit the ball to the desired target.

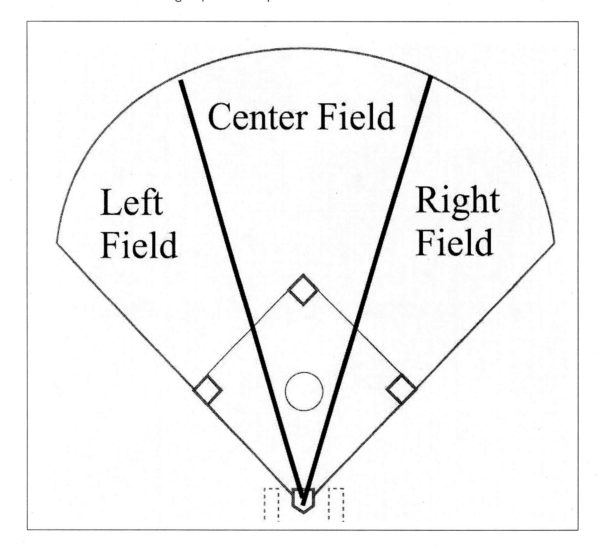

Drill #6: Two-Strike Drill, or 2+2+2

Objectives:
- Teaches the hitter how to face a two-strike situation
- Improves bat control
- Teaches the hitter how to make adjustments based on the count

Degree of Difficulty: 2B

Equipment Needed:
- Baseballs
- Bats
- Batting cage or baseball field
- Partner and screen

Description: A coach or partner pitches during this drill. The hitter approaches every pitch as if he is facing a two-strike situation. Make sure the hitter:
- Chokes up two inches on the bat.
- Moves two inches closer to the plate.
- Moves two inches toward the pitcher.

Coaching Points:
- With two strikes, the hitter needs to have the mindset that he is swinging at everything until he realizes it is a ball. In other words, the hitter needs to stay aggressive, but not so aggressive that he chases pitches out of the strike zone. This technique is sometimes called "passive aggressiveness." Many hitters get a called third strike because they are actually afraid of striking out. They become timid and freeze on good pitches.
- In a two-strike situation, the hitter should think about hitting the ball to the opposite field. The probabilities are that the pitcher will either work the outside corner or throw breaking pitches in this situation. So by thinking opposite field, the hitter is ready for those pitches and all he has to do is react if the pitch is inside. Most inside fastballs in this situation are for show (i.e., to move the hitter off the plate) and in most cases are balls. Remind hitters that some teams pitch backwards, meaning that the pitcher might start the hitter with off-speed pitches and try to finish him off with fastballs.
- The benefits of this approach outweigh the negatives. Even though the hitter will not generate as much power, he will be able to help the team more by putting the ball in play and getting on base more often.

Drill #7: Video Drill

Objective:
- Improves hitting mechanics by letting the hitter see what he is doing

Degree of Difficulty: 2B

Equipment Needed:
- Bat
- Baseballs
- Video camera
- One or two partners
- Optional: Right View Pro Digital Swing Analysis software

Description: To perform this drill, the hitter goes through his hitting process while a partner videotapes him from three different angles: front, back, and side. Have the hitter study the behavior of his head, stride, alignment, front-leg firmness, balance, shoulder position, arm extension, etc. The best way to read the video is in slow motion, pausing at critical stages of the swing. To take your video analysis to the next level, you can use Right View Pro (www.rightviewpro.com), a hitting motion analysis software that allows you to compare your swing with some of the best Major League hitters.

Coaching Points:
- The hitter can ask his coach for help in studying the video or he can go to his local batting cage and find a professional coach to help him.
- Major League players are given two videos at the end of the season—one with all their at bats and one with only their hits. Many hitters only like to see what they do when they do well, while others want to see the difference in their approach when they struggle and when they are successful.
- The hitter can start building a little database of swings by partnering with one of his teammates or having a parent videotape every at bat. After a while, he will have a good collection of his at bats and will be able to know what he does when he swings properly.

3

Drills to Put You in a Position to Swing with Power

Drill #8: Pull Bat Up with Grip

Objective:
• Shows the hitter if he has a proper and flexible grip

Degree of Difficulty: 1B

Equipment Needed:
• Bat
• A coach or adult

Description: The hitter takes his normal stance. A coach then grabs the bat head and pulls the bat upward to the sky. If the hitter has proper hand alignment and the elbows are down, he will resist the coach only with his arms. If the elbows are up or if the hitter is not properly gripping the bat, the coach will easily pull the bat up and the hitter will resist mostly with his shoulders, creating a lot of extra tension.

Coaching Points:
• This drill could help coaches show a hitter how to relax his upper-body muscles and improve his grip and arm position.
• This drill also shows a hitter how much more easily he can pull the bat down to start the swing when his arms are in the proper hitting position.

Drill #9: "Click It" Grip

Objectives:
- Improves the hitter's grip
- Improves contact impact
- Shortens the swing by putting the arms in the proper position

Degree of Difficulty: 1B

Equipment Needed:
- Bat
- Baseballs
- Partner and screen
- Batting cage

Description: In this drill, the hitter takes his swings after adjusting his grip on the bat. Most kids grow up gripping the bat with the fat part of the top hand resting on the thumb of the bottom hand. Instead, it should rest in between the thumb and the index finger. Teach the hitter to hold the bat correctly by having him turn the top hand until it passes over the last knuckle of the thumb and he feels the fat part of the top hand "click" into place.

Coaching Point:
- Changing the grip is uncomfortable, but doing this drill is worth the effort. The benefits of improving the swing should compensate for any discomfort.

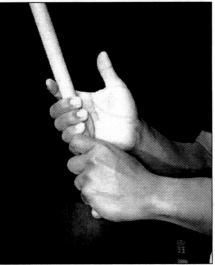

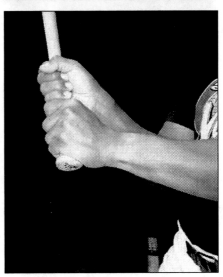

Drill #10: Jump and Land in the Athletic Position

Objective:
- Helps the hitter to find his strong and balanced position

Degree of Difficulty: 2B

Equipment Needed:
- Bat
- Baseballs
- Partner

Description: The hitter stands at the plate with his bat in his hands. Before the partner tosses the ball, the hitter jumps and lands with both feet planted on the ground. The partner checks the position to see if the hitter is in a strong position, then he tosses the ball to the hitter. The hitter must try to land in a position from which he will not fall. This stance is usually his athletic position, in which he can feel most of the weight on his thighs; the feet are planted on the ground and are positioned right outside the shoulders. The hitter can then try to start from that position as his regular hitting approach.

Coaching Points:
- This is a good beginner's drill.
- A strong foundation is essential for a strong swing. If the hitter is in weak position to hit, the whole approach will be weak.
- This drill is also good for hitters who are rising up during their swing. More than likely they are rising up because they have outgrown their stance or the stance is too narrow. This drill will likely demonstrate that the strongest position is usually wider than their normal position.

Drill #11: Proper Head Positioning

Objectives:
- Teaches the hitter to properly position his head/face during the stance
- Improves the ability to see the pitch

Degree of Difficulty: 1B

Equipment Needed:
- Bat
- Baseballs
- Partner
- Batting cage or baseball field
- Screen

Description: The hitter takes his stance at home plate. He then closes his front eye (i.e., the one closest to the pitcher) and finds the pitcher with the other eye. When he can see the pitcher with the back eye, he opens the front eye. He then keeps his head in that position, only moving it from there as he is tracking the ball to home plate. The hitter will be able to see the ball better and hit the ball more solidly.

Coaching Points:
- Many hitters tend to see the pitcher mostly with their front eye. In baseball terms, this is called peeking. When a hitter does this, he cannot focus on the ball as well and the eyes cannot give the brain the complete information it needs to help the hitter time and see the ball properly.
- Many hitters touch their chins to the front shoulder to put the head at the right position and to have the head at that position every time.
- The hitter needs to remember that two eyes are better than one if he wants to see the ball better and make good adjustments.
- This drill should only be done when the toss is coming front the direction of the pitcher, as during flips and batting practice. The hitter can also do dry swing or tee work by visualizing an imaginary pitcher in front of him.
- The hitter can also do this drill during the game until it becomes natural to him.

Drill #12: Bat on the Floor Alignment

Objectives:
- Teaches the hitter proper feet alignment
- Keeps the hitter squared to the plate

Degree of Difficulty: 2B

Equipment Needed:
- Two bats
- Baseballs
- Batting cage, baseball field, or open space
- Optional: Feeder, tee, screen

Description: The hitter uses one or two bats to check the position of his feet during the stance, the stride, and even on the follow-through. The hitter can stop at every phase of the swing and look down to his feet and bat(s) to check his alignment.

The following are three different ways to do this drill:

- The hitter places a bat in between the plate and where he stands, parallel to the plate with one end pointing to the pitcher. The hitter strives to keep his toes pointing to the bat while keeping himself squared. If the hitter strides toward or away from the bat, he will be able to notice and make the necessary adjustments. The hitter needs to work hard on keeping his balance throughout the swing by not getting himself out of his power position.

- To do the second version, the hitter needs two bats. He places one of the bats as described in version one and the other behind him. Both bats should be pointing to the pitcher. Enough space should exist between the bats so that the hitter to be able to do the hitting process properly. The hitter goes through the swing process, working hard on keeping himself squared to the plate.

- In the third version, the hitter also uses two bats. The hitter places one bat in between the plate and himself so he can check his alignment to the pitcher, and the other one perpendicular to the plate out in front of the hitting box, which will serve as a stride regulator. By doing this the hitter will have two objects to help him develop proper alignment and prevent overstriding. The hitter needs to make sure that the bat for the stride is not so close that he will step on it and risk injury. He should gradually bring the bat closer to him as his stride gets shorter. He needs to measure the length of the desired stride and place the bat a couple of inches past that point. At first, he should stride softly and mechanically until he has developed some muscle memory.

Coaching Points:

- The use of bats might be dangerous for some young players who stride toward the plate or overstride. If a hitter steps on the bat he can roll his ankle. A better choice for such hitters might be wooden boards.

- Version number two is a good drill for hitters who step away from the plate. If they keep doing that they will step on the bat behind them. As the hitter gets better he can close the distance of the bat behind him.

- The hitter needs to do a few swings without the bat(s) on the floor after doing the drill so he can transfer the feeling of the drill to his regular approach.

- Remember to look at the feet to check how he is landing and how he is performing all phases of the swing.

Drill #13: Rock Back

Objectives:
- Teaches the hitter to put the weight back before going forward
- Teaches the hitter to put and keep the weight on the backside
- Improves rhythm
- Improves weight shift

Degree of Difficulty: 2B

Equipment Needed:
- Baseballs
- Bat
- Feeder
- Screen
- Batting cage, baseball field, open space, or hitting net

Description: The hitter starts this drill standing at home plate with his knees flexed 20 to 25%. The hitter then rocks back until he feels about 70% of his weight on his back leg. The hitter does not take his stride until he has felt the weight on his back leg. The hands do not go back when the hitter is rocking back. After he feels the weight on his back leg, the hitter takes his stride. As the front foot is going forward, then the hands go back. The hitter lets the ball get deeper into the hitting zone and then, when he sees the ball at striking distance, the backside is thrown forcefully to the ball (hands and pivot at the same time).

The hitter starts rocking back when:
- The flipper or soft tosser is taking his arm back to toss the ball.
- The batting practice pitcher is lifting his leg up to throw the ball.
- The hitter thinks it is appropriate during tee work and dry swings.

Coaching Points:
- This drill, if done properly, will help the hitter to accomplish the following: Get his weight on his back leg, prepare the body for weight transfer, coil the body for power, and avoid jumping at the ball.
- This is a "timing and feeling" drill and should only be done during the off-season to teach the hitter to feel the weight on his backside. The hitter needs to do his normal swing after each set with this drill to transfer the feeling of the drill to his swing.
- The hitter needs to separate his hands from his stride by taking the hands back when the foot is going forward. The hands stay there until it is time to swing.

Drill #14: Stride Helper

Objectives:
- Prevents overstriding
- Teaches the hitter proper balance

Degree of Difficulty:
- Dry swings: 1B
- Tee work: 1B
- Soft toss: 2B
- Flips: 2B
- Batting practice: 3B

Equipment Needed:
- Bat
- Baseballs
- Batting cage
- Rope/flexibility cord/straps, etc.

Description: The idea of this drill is to put some kind of strap on both ankles with a rope in between to keep the hitter from overstriding.

Prior to doing this drill, you must follow these instructions to make the needed equipment:
- Rope: Tighten a knot at each end, making two holes big enough to fit over shoes. The distance between the holes should be as far as the hitter wants to stride (to protect the ankles, the hitter can add a piece of the foam).
- Bag straps: These straps can be used by forming loops with the end hooks that fit around the ankles.

- Flexibility cord: These cords are sold at sporting goods stores or rehab centers. They come with the holes already in place at the ends of the cord. The hitter only needs to reduce the length of the middle cord to accommodate the length of the desired stride by tightening knots or taping the desired distance.
- Weight lifting wraps: Use two of the leather or nylon wraps used to tighten around the ankles when performing leg exercises at the gym. They are sold at sporting good stores and come with a hook to tighten the rope with. This option is the most comfortable, but the most expensive.

The hitter then puts each leg/ankle into one of the holes. He strides, making sure he plants the front foot before starting the swing (for separation). The rope won't allow the hitter to overstride, thereby creating muscle memory so he can do it naturally later.

Coaching Points:
- The hitter should first start with dry swings and move up to batting practice as he improves.
- Overstriding produces a longer swing.
- If overstriding persists, one thing that can be done is widening the stance more.
- The hitter should strive for a short and soft stride. Short stride = short swing.
- The hitter needs to be aware that he might lose his balance during this drill. He needs to try to do it softly so he does not fall.

Drill #15: Heavy Obstacle Stride Correction

Objectives:
- Prevents overstriding
- Improves balance
- Makes the hitter wait back
- Forces the hitter to keep the front foot closed

Degree of Difficulty:
- Dry swings: 1B
- Tee work: 2B
- Soft tosses/flips: 3B
- Batting practice: HR

Equipment Needed:
- Heavy object that can be put on the floor (sand bag, concrete block, tire, etc.)
- Bat
- Baseballs
- Batting cage or baseball field
- Optional: Tee, partner, screen

Description: The hitter sets a relatively heavy object on the floor, as far as he wants to stride, to correct overstriding. The hitter then takes his stance at home plate. He takes his stride, expecting to be held by the object. After he lands his foot, he swings the bat, hitting the ball where it is pitched, and keeps the front foot closed. As a result, the hitter will have a firmer front leg and a better weight shift. He will also avoid overstriding, drifting, and lunging.

Coaching Points:
- The object used must be heavy enough to prevent the front foot from going forward too far, as well as something that keeps the hitter's front foot closed and pointing to home plate throughout the swing. A sand bag is probably the best object for this drill. It is heavy enough to stop the foot, but also soft enough that it will not hurt the foot.
- For proper leg use during the swing the hitter can combine this drill with the Squish the Bug Drill (Drill #78) by placing a rolled piece of paper under the big toe and then squishing a bug. Combining these two drills will give the hitter the muscle memory he needs to develop proper lower-body mechanics. As with all other drills, the hitter should always try to imitate the feeling of the drill without having the obstacle in front of him. He can follow the 10 + 5 routine, which entails taking 10 swings as described in the drill followed by five normal swings to translate what's been learned to the hitter's usual swing.

Drill #16: Stride—Ankle Weight on the Back Foot

Objectives:
- Teaches the hitter to keep his weight back during the stride
- Prevents overstriding
- Teaches the hitter to pivot the back foot and develop power

Degree of Difficulty:
- Dry swings/tee work: 1B
- Soft toss/flips: 2B
- Batting practice/machine: 3B

Equipment Needed:
- Bat
- Baseball
- Ankle weight
- Partner
- Batting cage or baseball field

Description: This drill gives the hitter something concrete to feel as he is working on keeping the back heel on the ground during the stride and on shortening his stride. Put an ankle weight on the hitter's back ankle. If the hitter lifts the back heel during the stride, he will feel the resistance of the weight. This drill can also help the hitter learn how to pivot properly and develop a more explosive pivot by overloading as the hitter starts his swing.

Coaching Point:
- The hitter needs to use an ankle weight that is heavy enough to keep the heel down, but not so heavy that it prevents him from pivoting the back foot.

Drill #17: Stride—Ankle Weight on the Front Foot

Objectives:
- Teaches the hitter to land softly the front foot during the stride
- Prevents overstriding
- Teaches the hitter to stride properly

Degree of Difficulty:
- Dry swings/tee work: 1B
- Soft tosses/flips: 2B
- Batting practice: 3B

Equipment Needed:
- Ankle weight (5 lb. or heavier)
- Baseballs
- Bat
- Batting cage or baseball field
- Optional: Partner, tee, screen

Description: The hitter tightens an ankle weight around the front leg. The weight should be heavy enough to give the hitter some resistance, but not so heavy that he cannot lift the foot. The hitter takes his stance with the ankle weight on the front foot. He then takes his normal stride and tries to land on the big toe or with the foot flat. The purpose of the weight is to make the hitter aware of what he is doing during the stride, shorten his stride, and slow down his step to the pitcher so he can see the ball better and have more balance.

Coaching Points:
- The weight will slow the stride down, helping the hitter see and feel what he is doing. He will be able to see where the foot is landing and correct any problems.
- The hitter needs to pause for a count before he starts his swing. Remind the hitter to "step to swing" and not "step and swing." Stride, pause, and swing.
- The stride is a little overrated. Lifting the foot up and putting it back down can have the same results as a high kick. The stride is done to break the inertia, or lack of movement, of the stance and put the hitter in the launching position ready to hit. The length of the step has nothing to do with how hard the hitter will hit the ball. Actually, a short and consistent stride means faster hands. Soft and short to the ball make for a better hitter. When the stride is too long, the hitter tends to lunge, drift, and lose his leg power because the back leg collapses. When the stride is too fast, it makes the hitter commit too soon. It prevents the hitter from seeing the ball well and he becomes susceptible to off-speed pitches.
- The hitter can do any of the hitting drills with the weight on his ankle. The more he repeats a drill, the more muscle memory he will gain by doing so. It takes many repetitions to get rid of a bad hitting habit.
- The hitter needs to warm up properly before doing this drill, especially his front leg.
- If an ankle weight is not available at school or at home, the hitter can buy one at any sporting good store or department store. The hitter can also make his own with a sanitary sock and sand. He ties one knot in the middle of the "sanie," then fills the sock with sand. Whe he thinks it is heavy enough, the hitter tightens another knot to close the sock. He can then tie the two ends of the sock around his ankle.

Drill #18: Carton—Beginner Stride Helper

Objectives:
- Teaches young hitters how to stride properly
- Shows hitters how they should stand at the plate

Degree of Difficulty:
- Tee work/dry swings: 1B
- Soft toss/flips: 2B

Equipment Needed:
- Carton
- A dark sharpie or marker
- Bat
- Tee
- Baseballs

Description: The coach or parent takes an old box and opens and flattens it. He then draws four things on it:
- Home plate
- Two shoe soles pointing to the plate and spread apart on the side that the hitter's stance would be. On the back shoe, the parent can draw a bug on the big toe and then have the hitter swing by squishing the bug.
- A third shoe sole a few inches away from the front sole illustrating the distance of the stride.
- A stride line between the soles and the plate to show the hitter that he should stand and stride in a straight line toward the pitcher.

The hitter then stands on the box with his feet on the two shoes pointing to the plate. He then takes his stride, trying to land on the sole drawn in front with the foot closed. The hitter is then taught to keep the feet apart from each other and at the same location during the swing.

This drill can also be performed indoors with a tee, using tape to mark the feet locations of the stance and stride (see photos).

Coaching Points:
- This drill can be done in the garage as the hitter is learning to use his legs during the swing.
- To make this drill more complete, the coach can put a concrete block at the front of the front foot and a sand bag at the side of the back foot to show the hitter how to use his legs properly.

Drill #19: Pole to Prevent Wrapping

Objectives:
- Eliminates the muscle memory of wrapping the bat
- Can help the hitter finish his swing

Degree of Difficulty:
- Dry swings: 1B
- Tee work: 2B
- Soft toss/flips: 3B

Equipment Needed:
- Pole, tree, or punching bag
- Optional: Bat and balls

Description: The hitter stands in front of a pole (or tree/punching bag) and takes his stance with the bat touching the pole. The hitter then takes his stride; the pole will stop the hitter from wrapping his bat behind his head. This drill can also teach hitters to finish their swings by having them aim to hit the outside of the pole at the end of the swing.

Coaching Points:
- The hitter can set up a tee in front of him if he wants a ball involved in this drill.
- The hitter can use an L-shaped screen (parallel to the plate) if he wants to do this with flips.
- If a pole is not available, you can stand behind the hitter at a distance far enough away that the hitter will not hit you with his swing. Resist the hitter with a bat and give the hitter the command for when to swing. As soon as you give the command, drop your bat and let the hitter finish his swing.

Drill #20: Wait, Wait, Now

Objectives:
- Improves the launching position
- Develops bat speed
- Improves reaction time
- Teaches the hitter to stay back and let the ball get deeper into the hitting zone
- Improves separation of the stride and the hands

Degree of Difficulty:
- Soft toss: 2B
- Flips: 3B

Equipment Needed:
- Bat
- Baseballs
- Batting cage, hitting net, baseball field, or open space
- Partner

Description: The person feeding the ball has a major role in the drill, so it is important that an experienced person assumes that position. The hitter stands at home plate while the feeder is at a 45-degree angle in front of him (i.e., in the soft toss position). The feeder tosses the ball and says "wait, wait", while the hitter waits for the ball. Then, when the feeder thinks it is time for the hitter to swing, he yells "now!" The hitter reacts and hits the ball hard into the net.

The feeder needs to be as realistic as possible, but at the same time challenge the hitter to wait as long as he can before he swings. The longer the hitter waits, the better he will see the ball, thus improving contact. This will also help him avoid getting fooled as often by off-speed pitches. To keep the hitter from anticipating when to swing, the partner should occasionally not say "now." The hitter should take those tosses without swinging.

Coaching Points:
- This is a good drill for those who do not separate their hands from their stride (i.e., they bring the hands forward as they stride).
- There should always be a pause between the toss and the "now" (swing).
- The feeder needs to challenge the hitter, making him wait as long as possible.
- For younger hitters, use flips; more experienced hitters can use the soft toss.

Drill #21: Step, Twist, and Swing

Objectives:
- Teaches the hitter to use his hands properly during the swing
- Improves separation
- Teaches the hitter to use his front foot and improves body rhythm

Degree of Difficulty: 2B

Equipment Needed:
- Bat
- Baseballs
- Batting cage, net, or field

Description: The hitter begins this drill behind home plate, with his whole body facing where the pitcher would be (perpendicular to the plate) and his bat either on the back shoulder or in front of him. He takes a small step forward with the foot closest to the plate, and then does a half circle step with the other leg. That foot needs to land where it usually lands after he strides. As the foot is going forward, the hands go back to their launching position. Whoever is doing the toss or the flip has to wait until the hitter has landed the front foot to throw the ball. If this drill is being performed during tee practice, make sure there is a small separation between the stride and when the hands start the downward path to the ball.

Coaching Points:
- This drill can be performed with either soft tosses or flips.
- The hitter needs to land softly and use his hands (land on the toes of the front foot to stay square and slow everything down).
- Have the hitter maintain a firm front foot (this prevents the body from drifting).
- The feeder should take necessary precautions to protect himself.

Drill #22: Fungo to Determine Hitting Position

Objectives:
- Allows the hitter to find his true launching position
- Teaches the hitter to take the hands back and load
- Eliminates extra movements from the swing

Degree of Difficulty: 2B

Equipment Needed:
- Bat or fungo
- Baseballs
- Batting cage or baseball field

Description: The hitter can use a fungo or his regular bat and he can either hit grounders to a fielder or in front of a net. The idea is for the hitter to hit grounders to determine the position of his hands when in the launching position. The hitter tosses the ball to himself with the front hand and quickly brings that hand back to the bat, takes his hands back to load, and then hits the ball. While doing a few repetitions of this drill, the hitter should take mental notes regarding where his hands are going before he swings down to hit the ball. After a few swings, the hitter takes his regular swing, focusing on taking his hands back to his launching position right away. The hitter then takes a few swings involving a ball and tries to give his hands the muscle memory they need to go right away to that point so the swing works efficiently and without extra movements.

Coaching Points:
- The hitter does not need to overswing. He needs to work on nice easy swings with the fungo and try to imitate his regular approach on his swing
- The hitter will notice that when he hits fungoes the hands go behind the back shoulder and are kept high, so it is easy to take the bat head right to the ball. He needs to take the same approach during his regular swing.

Drill #23: Separation—Fake a Toss

Objectives:
- Teaches the hitter to separate his stride both from his hands and from the swing
- Helps the hitter develop a strong launching position
- Allows the hitter to see the ball better
- Teaches the hitter to stay and wait back

Degree of Difficulty:
- Soft tosses: 2B
- Flips: 2B
- Batting practice: 3B

Equipment Needed:
- Baseballs
- Bat
- Partner
- Batting cage or baseball field
- Screen

Description: The hitter takes his stance at home plate. The partner protects himself behind a screen in the direction of the pitcher 15 to 20 feet away in a flip position. The partner then fakes a toss. The hitter takes his stride and separates his hands from his front foot as if the partner is actually tossing the ball. The hitter acts as if he is taking the pitch properly, keeping his hands back and going to his balanced athletic position. The partner reloads and this time tosses the ball. The hitter waits back and hits the ball according to where it is pitched. To keep the hitter on his toes, the partner needs to occasionally toss the ball when he is supposed to be faking the toss. That way, the hitter will work on attaining a good hitting position with every pitch.

Coaching Points:
- The key to performing this drill well is that the hitter has a strong launching position. The front foot is on the big toe. The back foot is flat on the ground. The knees are slightly bent, with the front knee inside the front foot. The hands are back and both elbows are pointing to the ground. Both eyes on the ball.
- Though this drill is intended for underhand flips, the hitter can start this drill with soft toss and move all the way up to batting practice.
- When the hitter pauses, the partner can give him enough time to check his launching position before tossing the ball. If the hitter does not like it, he can change it.
- This drill will help the hitter to wait back longer, while keeping his power and avoiding getting fooled by off-speed pitches as often.

Step, stop and wait

Drill #24: Top Hand Back—Stop Wrapping the Bat

Objectives:
- Helps the hitter avoid "wrapping" the bat behind his head
- Shortens and quickens the swing by eliminating extra movements
- Puts the hands in the proper launching position

Degree of Difficulty:
- Dry swings/tee work: 1B
- Soft tosses/flips: 2B
- Batting practice: 3B

Equipment Needed:
- Baseballs
- Bat
- Batting cage or a baseball field
- Partner and screen
- Optional: Tee

Description: The hitter takes his stance at home plate and grips the bat as usual. The hitter opens his bottom hand up, but keeps the palm touching the bat. He then goes through his normal hitting process starting with the stride. He should take his hands back by taking the top hand back, which is gripping the bat (remember, he is just touching the bat with the palm of the bottom hand). After the hitter lands his stride, he then grips the bat with the bottom hand and prepares himself to swing the bat.

Remind the hitter that the key to successfully taking the hands back is for him to be able to take the top hand back. Ideally, both hands will be taken back as at unit, and this drill can give the hitter the muscle memory he needs to accomplish that. The hands should be taken farther back than the back shoulder; there should be a space between the shoulder and the hands. Most importantly, after the hitter takes his hands back, he needs to keep them back until the ball is at striking distance. Instead of letting the bat drop behind his head, the hitter should keep the bat head above his head

Coaching Points:
- Wrapping the bat behind the head occurs when the hitter thinks he has taken his hands back, but in truth has only taken his bottom hand back and kept the top hand in the same place, making the bat collapse behind his head. Because the hitter feels and sees his bottom arm going back, he believes that he is accomplishing the separation of the hands and the stride, but in actuality his bat goes behind the head, making the swing path to the ball longer.
- The hitter needs to start this drill using a tee. The hitter takes his stride, stops, checks his body's position, and, when he feels everything is in the right place, takes his swing.
- After the hitter feels comfortable with this drill, he can increase the level of difficulty of the drill.
- A little space should be present between the back shoulder and the hands. This is very important.

Drill #25: Two Hands Toss to a Net

Objectives:
- Improves trigger action
- Teaches the hitter to throw his hands to the ball
- Improves arm extension on contact
- Improves bat speed

Degree of Difficulty: 2B

Equipment Needed:
- A ball (or a bucket of balls)
- Batting cage or hitting net

Description: The hitter holds a baseball with both hands. He then takes his hands to where he normally holds his bat during his stance. The idea is to throw the ball into the net as if he is taking a swing. The hitter:
- Takes his stride
- Takes his hands back
- Pauses on separation (front foot forward, hands back)
- Forcefully tosses the ball to the net, letting the ball go where contact would have been made (middle of the net)
- Mimics his regular follow-through

Each hitter should toss the ball 10 times then swing the bat five times to keep the feeling of throwing the hands.

Coaching Points:
- The hitter needs to toss the ball into the net as hard as possible.
- The hitter needs to remember to do the five steps of the hitting process (stance, stride, swing, contact, and follow-through) using the ball.
- Taking the ball back before throwing it will teach the hitter to recoil and trigger. This will improve his bat speed.
- The hitter needs to work on visualizing hitting different pitch locations.
- The hitter should do this drill at his convenience and when practicing by himself.
- The hitter needs to warm up his arms before doing this drill.

Drill #26: Coach Mirror

Objectives:
- Provides a model of good hitting technique for the hitter to emulate
- Eliminates mechanical flaws during the stance, stride, and launching position
- Provides a visual means of learning new hitting mechanics

Degree of Difficulty: 2B

Equipment Needed:
- Baseballs
- Tee
- Bat
- Batting cage or hitting net
- Partner (preferably a coach)
- Optional: Feeder, screen

Description: The hitter stands at home plate and the coach stands at the other side of the plate facing him. If the hitter is right-handed, the coach stands left-handed. The coach shows what he wants the hitter to accomplish and the hitter mimics what he is doing.

Coaching Points:
- The idea of this drill is to help a hitter who has mechanical flaws in his stance, stride, or launching position by having the hitter imitate a coach or player that knows the right mechanics.
- Some examples of mechanics that can be targeted are landing the stride on the big toe and staying up; maintaining proper separation of the stride and the hands; reaching the proper launching position, etc.
- This is a good drill to do with beginners and with hitters who are very visual.
- The coach or player can also show the hitter what he is doing wrong so the hitter actually sees his mistakes.
- Only dry swings and tee work should be used for this drill. Using a live ball might put the coach or player in some kind of danger.
- The hitter should watch the coach complete his swing before turning his head in the direction of the pitcher and swinging the bat.

4

Drills to Discipline the Head and See the Ball Better

Objectives:
- Develops power
- Improves trigger action (take hands back)
- Improves reaction time
- Improves bat control
- Develops hand-eye coordination
- Disciplines the hitter to wait longer (off-speed work)

Degree of Difficulty: 2B

Equipment Needed:
- Bat
- Tennis balls
- Batting cage, baseball field, or open space

Description: The hitter stands a couple of steps off home plate. He holds a tennis ball with his bottom hand and a bat with his top hand. The hitter then tosses the ball underhand strongly enough that it reaches the strike zone when it bounces in front of him. After he lets go of the ball, the hitter takes a crossover step to load up to hit the ball (i.e., the back foot goes in front of the front foot, then the front foot goes behind the back foot and lands where the stride would regularly land at home plate). As the ball is coming up, the hitter takes a powerful swing, pushing the ball away from him. The hitter should try to hit a line drive home run with every swing.

Coaching Points:
- For this drill to work well, the front foot needs to be firm throughout the swing, but especially right after landing the crossover step.
- When hitting the ball, the hitter should think "hands in front, body back" for proper weight shifting and rotational power.
- When doing this drill, many hitters tend to uppercut. The hitter needs to always think down, not up.

Drill #28: Glove Head—Balanced Swing

Objectives:
- Stabilizes the head during the swing
- Improves balance
- Improves the ability to see the ball

Degree of Difficulty:
- Dry swings/tee work: 2B
- Soft tosses/flips: 3B
- Batting practice: HR

Equipment Needed:
- Glove
- Helmet
- Baseballs
- Bat
- Batting cage or baseball field
- Optional: Tee

Description: The hitter puts his glove on his head as if the glove is catching the head. The hitter then goes through his swing without letting the glove fall off his head. He needs to swing hard but with control, trying to keep his head still throughout the swing so the glove does not move. To make this drill more challenging, the hitter can wear a helmet beneath the glove.

Coaching Points:
- The hitter can compete with a friend to see who takes the most swings without dropping the glove on the ground.
- The hitter should start this drill with dry swings and then move up to more challenging drills.
- The hitter needs to keep the head down and stable while trying to see the ball hit the bat and keeping the eyes on the contact area after he has hit the ball.

Drill #29: Follow the Ball into the Glove

Objectives:
• Improves the ability to see the ball
• Teaches the hitter to keep the head down
• Improves balance and keeps the body back

Degree of Difficulty: HR

Equipment Needed:
• Bat
• Baseballs
• A batting practice pitcher and a catcher
• Baseball field or batting cage

Description: The hitter takes his stance at home plate. The idea is for the hitter to take one pitch and follow the ball all the way to the glove, and then swing at the next pitch while doing the same. If the hitter wants, he can tell the catcher if the pitch is a ball or strike and see if the catcher agrees with his understanding of the strike zone.

The hitter needs to try to track the ball all the way to the contact area and try to see the ball hit the bat. The hitter needs to keep the head down with his eyes on the contact area even after he has hit the ball.

Coaching Point:
• The hitter might also want to ask the batting practice pitcher to throw different pitches and to different locations to simulate a game. The more he practices in a game-like situation, the more prepared he will be for the real game.

Drill #30: Head Down Tee Work

Objectives:
- Teaches the hitter to keep the head down during and after contact
- Improves balance and arm extension
- Improves the ability to see the ball

Degree of Difficulty: 2B

Equipment Needed:
- Tee
- Bat
- Baseballs
- Batting cage or baseball field
- Optional: Partner

Description: The hitter swings the bat and hits the ball off the tee, but after he hits it he keeps his eyes on top of the tee where the ball was placed. To challenge himself, the hitter can have a partner place a coin underneath the ball. The hitter then hits the ball and has to tell the partner if the coin was heads or tails. If the hitter is wrong, he needs to do five push-ups.

Coaching Points:
- The hitter can stop after his stride to check his power position before he hits the ball. If can then make adjustments before hitting the ball.
- The ball should be placed with the seams perpendicular to the ground. The hitter then hits the ball by aiming to hit the one closest to him, to keep the swing short.
- If a partner is not available, the hitter can place the coin down himself without looking.
- Another option, if coins are not available, is to have the partner set his hand in a fist at about a 45-degree angle from the ball in front of the hitter. The hitter then hits the ball and keeps his head down as the partner flashes a number with his fingers as the hitter is making contact.

Drill #31: Follow the Ball

Objectives:
- Teaches the hitter to keep the eyes on the ball
- Develops concentration and focus

Degree of Difficulty: 1B

Equipment Needed:
- Baseballs
- Bat
- Open space, baseball field, or batting cage
- Coach or parent

Description: To begin the drill, the coach tells the hitter to only look at the ball. Before tossing the ball, the coach moves the ball around, making the hitter follow the ball (many young hitters will tend to make eye contact with the coach). When the adult sees that the hitter's eyes are following the ball, he then tosses a soft strike to the hitter, always reminding him to see the ball hit the bat.

Coaching Points:
- This drill is designed for younger hitters who have a hard time tracking the ball or learning to hit live pitching. This drill can be done with a plastic ball and bat.
- Older hitters can also do this drill during flips, though the feeder needs to make sure that he is behind the screen at all times so he does not get hit by a ball.
- The coach can move the ball through different patterns in front of his body before he tosses the ball.

Drill #32: Watching Pitchers Working on the Side

Objectives:
- Allows the hitter to get timing work from a regular pitcher
- Allows the hitter to see different pitches and their trajectories
- Teaches the hitter to see the ball all the way
- Improves knowledge of the strike zone
- Helps the hitter develop a strong launching position

Degree of Difficulty: 1B

Equipment Needed:
- Bat or bat handle
- Pitcher and catcher practicing on the side

Description: The hitter stands at home plate with his regular stance and reacts to the pitch without actually swinging the bat (he takes his stride, but flinches to the ball without swinging). The hitter could ask the pitcher to throw a certain pitch, especially if he has problems hitting it. Also, he could learn the strike zone by either calling balls and strikes and asking the catcher if he agrees or by simply having the catcher act as an umpire.

Coaching Points:
- What seems to be a simple drill could be of great help to a hitter, especially if he has not played for a while and needs to get his timing in a hurry.
- Even though the hitter is not swinging, younger hitters should use a helmet. It's better to be safe than sorry, especially when less experienced pitchers are throwing.
- The hitter can use a bat handle or short PVC pipe to dry swing to the pitch. The catcher decides whether or not the hitter swung at a good pitch.

Drill #33: Hitting Colored Balls

Objectives:
- Improves concentration
- Improves hand-eye coordination
- Helps the hitter keep his eyes on the ball longer
- Provides muscle memory for keeping the head down

Degree of Difficulty: 2B

Equipment Needed:
- Balls (baseball, tennis, etc.)
- Different color paints or permanent markers
- Bat
- Batting cage
- Partner

Description:
- The hitter takes 10 balls (or as many as you can afford to paint) and does the following:

- Paint three balls with one color (e.g., one red, one black, and one blue).
- Color three balls half one color and half another.
- Color three balls with four colors, using the four big white spots on the ball as a guide.
- Leave one ball white.

Someone then soft tosses or flips these balls to him. The hitter has to identify the color or colors of all of the balls, not just the one he hits. To make the drill more challenging, the hitter can try to name what color he actually hit, and not all the colors he sees.

Coaching Points:
- To do this drill properly the hitter needs to keep his head down.
- Tell the hitter to slow himself down, so he can see the ball better.
- Whoever is flipping the balls should remain behind the screen at all times.

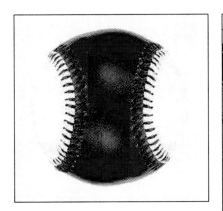

Drill #34: Pom Poms—See the Ball

Objectives:
- Improves the way the hitter sees the ball
- Improves hand-eye coordination and focus

Degree of Difficulty: 3B

Equipment Needed:
- Pom poms
- Bat, fungo, or broomstick
- Open space
- Partner

Description: The partner can toss the pom poms either under- or overhand. The hitter needs to quiet his head to see the pom poms better and avoid swinging and missing as often.

Coaching Points:
- The hitter needs a bag of "pom poms" that kids use for crafts; they can be bought at any department or craft store. The hitter can also use mini-marshmallows if pom poms are not available.
- The more colors of pom poms used, the better. The hitter can tell the partner what color he just hit.
- This drill is safer than hitting corn seeds or beans because the partner's eyes are in less danger of being hit, and if the pom pom hits him it will not sting.
- The hitter can start with his regular bat. As he improves, he can use a fungo, then a broomstick. For an even tougher drill the hitter can close one eye or use an eye patch.

Drill #35: Hitting Wiffle® Balls

Objectives:
- Improves the way the hitter sees the ball
- Develops concentration and hand-eye coordination
- Improves ball tracking
- Teaches the hitter to wait back to hit off-speed pitches and breaking balls

Degree of Difficulty: 2B

Equipment Needed:
- Wiffle balls (plastic ball with holes)
- Bat
- Partner

Description: The hitter takes batting practice as the partner pitches the Wiffle balls and tries to make the ball move and change locations.

Coaching Points:
- Wiffle balls are relatively cheap and are readily available in any department store or sporting goods store. Hitters can use either of two sizes: regular baseball size and a more challenging golf ball size. Because of the holes in the ball, the wind makes the ball move all over the place. It is like hitting a knuckleball or change up.
- Because the balls don't carry very far, they allow the hitters to do their work either inside during the winter months or outside when space is limited.
- The hitter needs to wait back and be patient.
- Off-speed pitches are seldom worked during batting practice, so this drill could help the hitter complete his hitting practice program.

Drill #36: See the Ball, Hit the Ball

Objectives:
- Teaches the hitter to see the ball better during the swing
- Improves concentration, focus, and hand-eye coordination
- Improves the way the hitter tracks the ball

Degree of Difficulty:
- Soft tosses: 2B
- Flips: 2B
- Batting practice: 3B

Equipment Needed:
- Baseballs
- Bat
- Partner
- Batting cage or baseball field
- Screen

Description: The hitter takes batting practice while making a conscious effort to see the ball hit the bat during contact. It might not be possible to actually see the ball hit the bat, but practicing this way will help the hitter see the ball better and keep his head down during contact, which gives him better balance during the swing. After he hits the ball, the hitter tries to keep his eyes on the contact area. Once he makes contact, and after the back shoulder hits the chin, he should look to see where the ball goes or let the first base coach help him find it. A baseball can also be set at home plate. When the hitter finishes his swing, he finds the ball at home plate.

Coaching Points:
- Advise the hitter to avoid moving his head until the back shoulder has hit the chin.
- By keeping his head down, the hitter will not only have better balance throughout the swing, but he will also have a shorter swing to the ball.
- The hitter cannot let the head fly over the front shoulder or let the eyes follow the ball after he hits it. The upper body follows the head, so by keeping the head down on contact, he keeps his swing simple and efficient. The front shoulder and the chin do not work together. As the front shoulder moves outwardly, the chin goes in the opposite direction toward the back shoulder.
- The better tracking of the ball will help the hitter see the late breaks of off-speed pitches, helping him to avoid getting fooled as often and to react accordingly to each pitch.
- The tosser should throw pitches in all areas of the strike zone.

Drill #37: Breaking Ball Batting Practice

Objectives:
- Teaches the hitter to hit breaking balls
- Teaches the hitter to stay back and keep the weight back
- Improves hand-eye coordination
- Allows the hitter to practice in game-like conditions

Degree of Difficulty: 3B

Equipment Needed:
- Bat
- Baseballs
- Coach or partner
- Baseball field or batting cage

Description: During this drill, the hitter sees mostly breaking balls instead of nice batting-practice fastballs. The coach or partner throws curveballs and sliders, mixing in an occasional fastball.

Coaching Points:
- Most hitters do not hit breaking pitches well, not because they are bad breaking ball hitters but because they do not practice hitting them often enough.
- To hit a curveball, the hitter needs to do the following:
    - ✓ Do not "hang." The hitter should not slow down because of the speed of the pitch; instead, he should put the foot down as if a fastball is coming and then wait back a little bit longer.
    - ✓ Keep the hands back. The hitter will get fooled once in a while, but he needs to learn to be fooled only with his front side while keeping the hands back behind the back shoulder. Most hitters get fooled and bring their hands to the body and end up just pushing the ball with no power.
    - ✓ See the ball hit the bat. The hitter should not give up on the ball, but instead follow the ball all the way to contact.
- Most problems hitting a curveball occur because the hitter uses the front shoulder and the head together instead of keeping the head in longer.
- To hit a breaking pitch, the hitter needs to think of going with the rotation. If the rotation goes away from him, he should hit the ball the other way. If the rotation is coming to him he can and should pull the ones that are middle-in, but he needs to make sure he stays inside the ball instead of going around it. For pitches middle-away, he should try to hit the ball back to the pitcher or to the opposite field.
- The hitter needs to always stay inside the ball and wait back at his launching position. He should look for a fastball and stay back to get the benefits of the drill. Even though he knows that a breaking pitch is coming, he should not perform as if he is guessing for it. This is the reason why the pitcher should occasionally throw a fastball to keep the hitter honest.

Drill #38: Release Point

Objectives:
- Improves how quickly the hitter finds the ball at the release point
- Improves ball tracking

Degree of Difficulty:
- Taking the pitch: 1B
- Batting practice with a swing: 2B

Equipment needed:
- Bat
- Baseballs
- Partner
- Batting cage/L screen

Description: This drill can be done in two different ways—by taking the pitch or swinging. The partner tosses the ball and as soon as the hitter sees the ball in the air, he yells "ball!" The idea is to diminish the reaction time between the pitcher letting go of the ball and the hitter picking it up.

Coaching Points:
- To make this drill more challenging, the partner can switch release points or throw different pitches.
- The hitter can also say, "There it is." This seems to focus the hitter even more on the ball.

Drill #39: Ball Recognition

Objectives:
- Improves tracking
- Improves speed of recognition (how fast the hitter picks the ball from the hand)

Degree of Difficulty:
- Soft toss and flips: 2B
- Batting practice: 3B

Equipment Needed:
- Different color Wiffle balls or different types of balls (tennis, machine balls, regular baseballs, and even softballs).
- Bat
- Batting cage
- Partner

Description: The partner has either different colored Wiffle balls or at least two different types of balls. The partner then says a color or a type of ball. He then tosses any ball, but the hitter can only swing at the color or type of ball the partner announced. He should take all other pitches.

Coaching Points:
- The partner says one color or type of ball before each toss. He should also hide the ball in a way that the hitter will not see it until it is coming out of his hand.
- This is a very demanding drill, but it will help the hitter to see the ball better, pick it up sooner, and not miss his pitch.

Drill #40: Colored Wiffle Balls

Objectives:
- Improves tracking
- Improves bat control
- Improves mental clarity and decision-making skills

Degree of Difficulty: HR

Equipment Needed:
- Different colored Wiffle balls or different type of balls (baseballs, softballs, tennis balls, machine balls, Wiffle balls, etc.)
- Bat
- Batting cage
- Partner

Description: The partner has either three different colored Wiffle balls or three types of balls (e.g., baseballs, machine rubber balls, and tennis balls). The partner tells the hitter one of two ways of doing this drill:
- The hitter has to hit one color or type of ball to his pull side, another to the middle of the field, and the third to the opposite field.
- The hitter has to hit one color or type of ball to his pull side; another to the opposite field, and let the third go without swinging.

Coaching Points:
- This is an extreme vision and bat-control drill.
- The key is for the player to find the ball as quickly as possible and recognize it early.

RED
Opposite Field

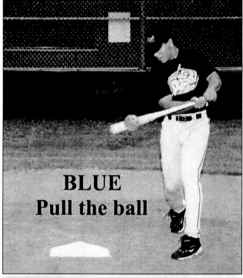

BLUE
Pull the ball

WHITE
Take the pitch

Drill #41: 1, 2, 3 Release to Contact

Objectives:
• Teaches the hitter to track the ball
• Improves timing and contact

Degree of Difficulty:
• Flips: 2B
• Batting practice/batting machine: 3B

Equipment Needed:
• Ball
• Baseballs
• Batting cage
• Partner
• Optional: Batting machine

Description: The hitter counts from one to three as follows: "one" as the batting practice pitcher releases the ball, "two" while the ball is on the way to the plate, and "three" as he starts his swing. Sometimes the "three" will be quicker than normal, especially with hard fastballs.

Coaching Points:
• This is a good timing drill. It is a very simple drill, but one that has the potential to help any hitter concentrate on the ball, see the ball better, and make better contact.
• The hitter needs to make sure to let the ball get deep into the hitting zone.
• The hitter can eventually use this drill as his normal hitting approach during the game.

Drill #42: The Strikeout Game

Objectives:
• Gives young players a way to play more baseball
• Lets the hitter see different pitches and gives him game-like practice

Degree of Difficulty: 2B

Equipment Needed:
• Rubber ball or tennis ball
• Bat
• Concrete block
• Open space
• Partner

Description: The hitter draws or sets in tape a strike zone on a concrete fence or wall. The partner, using a rubber ball or tennis ball, tries to strike the hitter out. The partner can also get an out if he catches a fly ball or ground ball. The players decide how many outs and how many innings to play. As the players get more comfortable doing this drill, they can incorporate running the bases (only first and second) to make it more like a real baseball game.

Coaching Point:
• The players need to set the foul lines before the game. Also, a base hit line should be set; this is a line between the hitter and the pitcher that the ball needs to go over to be a hit.

Drill #43: Tennis Ball on the Chin

Objectives:
• Teaches the hitter to keep the head down
• Positions the head properly during the stride

Degree of Difficulty:
• Dry swings/tee work: 2B
• Soft toss/flips: 2B
• Batting practice: 3B

Equipment Needed:
• Bat
• Baseball
• Tennis ball or rubber ball
• Partner
• Optional: Tee

Description: The hitter places a tennis ball between his chin and the front of the front shoulder. The hitter then goes through his swing process, trying to keep the tennis ball in place while tracking the pitched ball and as he begins to take the bat to the ball. As the hitter starts the swing, the tennis ball will automatically fall. If the ball drops between the arms and lands by the front foot, the drill was performed properly. If the ball drops outside the front foot or seems to be stuck between the chin and shoulder, then the hitter's head flew out prematurely.

Coaching Points:
• This drill is done to keep the head in the right position during the stance, stride, and launching position and to see if the head is staying down or flying away during the swing.
• The hitter can put the ball under his T-shirt if he does not want to drop it. He can also put another ball under the T-shirt at the back shoulder to see if he is finishing the swing properly.

5

Drills to Improve the Mechanics of the Swing Path

Drill #44: Starting the Swing with Maximum Power

Objectives:
- Improves power
- Improves bat speed
- Improves swing intensity and makes the swing more compact

Degree of Difficulty:
- Dry swings/tee work: 2B
- Soft toss/flips: 3B

Equipment Needed:
- Bat
- Balls
- Batting cage or baseball field

Description: The goal of this drill is to do four different tasks simultaneously. By doing so, the hitter will generate maximum power during the swing.

- Snap the front knee (the front knee is flexed and the proper rotation firms it up)
- Pivot the back heel backward (on the big toe)
- Pull the hands to the ball (the back elbow goes in front of the chest)
- Try to see the ball hit the bat

Coaching Points:
- The hitter can think about each of these tasks as 25% of his power. If he does not do one aspect properly, he will only be using about 75% of his power.
- The focus of this drill should be on teaching hitters to start the swing with maximum power.
- Remind the hitter to exhale at the beginning of the swing.
- The hitter can start this drill by mastering each phase one at time and start combining them until the four can be done without thinking.

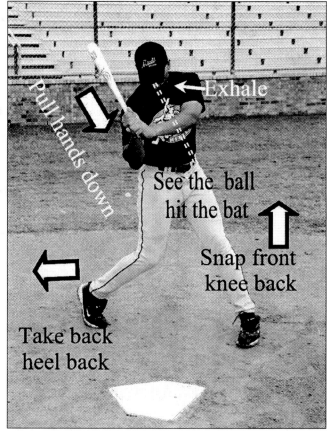

Drill #45: Front Arm Tight Swing

Objectives:
- Helps the hitter avoid taking the front elbow to the pitcher ("chicken wing")
- Gives the hitter muscle memory to keep the swing compact and the arms close to the body
- Improves body rotation

Degree of Difficulty:
- Dry swings/tee work: 2B
- Soft toss/flips: 3B

Equipment Needed:
- Belt
- Bat
- Baseballs
- Batting cage
- Optional: Tee, partner

Description: The hitter or a partner tightens a baseball uniform belt around the hitter's front upper arm and the upper body. The hitter then swings, keeping the front arm close to the body all the way through the swing. The back arm needs to finish the swing by pushing through the ball. The hitter needs to keep the body tall and the head still.

Coaching Points:
- The hitter needs to swing the bat a few times after the drill without the belt to transfer the feeling of compactness to his swing.
- The key of this drill is to keep the head still and the body back during the swing.

Drill #46: Backside Drill

Objectives:
- Improves the launching position
- Teaches the hitter to wait back on the ball
- Maximizes power
- Helps the hitter swing harder and transfer his weight properly

Degree of Difficulty:
- Dry swings: 1B
- Tee work: 1B
- Soft tosses: 2B
- Flips: 2B
- Batting practice: 3B

Equipment Needed:
- Baseballs
- Bat
- Optional: Partner

Description: During this drill the hitter makes a conscious effort to throw his hands to the ball and pivot the back foot at the same time. This action will make the hitter's backside explosively come forward to the ball and in unison.

Coaching Points:
- This is a great drill that teaches the hitter to wait back on the ball longer and to utilize his total power.
- This drill sounds easy to do, but it is not. It requires coordination and hard work. Most hitters have a two-part swing. The upper body and the lower body do what they are supposed to, but at different times. The hands and the back leg are in a race, and the hands will always play catch up. But if the hands and the back leg start at the same time the timing will be almost always perfect. The hitter will be able to wait longer on the ball, the swing will look cleaner because no wasted movements are present, and the hitter will have more power.
- The lower body leaving the upper body behind is called "quick hip." The upper body leaving the lower body behind is called "pulling off the ball" or "opening the front shoulder too soon."
- The harder the hitter wants to hit the ball, the harder he needs to push down when he is pivoting the back foot.
- Pivoting the back foot and throwing the hands at the same time will help the hitter wait a bit longer on the ball and help him to avoid committing too soon, letting him see the ball longer and better.
- This drill will also help the hitter stay back on his backside, thereby allowing to keep his power back longer and use his hands better because the body will not get in the way of the swing.
- The hitter should take his hands behind the back shoulder and back foot. Then he can throw them explosively to the ball to generate power and bat speed.

Drill #47: Hit the Hat

Objectives:
- Shortens the hitter's swing
- Forces the hitter to take the bat head right to the ball

Degree of Difficulty:
- Tee work: 2B
- Flips: 3B
- Batting practice: 3B

Equipment Needed:
- Bat
- Baseballs
- Hat or glove
- Optional: Tee

Description: The hitter places a hat, glove, or any other unbreakable object between him and the pitcher. The hitter then swings aiming to hit the object. The hitter should only do this drill with the ball coming from the pitcher's direction or with tee work if he is working by himself (he can also self-toss the ball).

Coaching Points:
- The object will give the hitter a purpose, and indirectly will help him shorten his swing.
- After he has the feeling of taking the bat head right to the ball, the hitter can remove the object and mimic the feeling of the drill without the object being placed in front of him.

Drill #48: Two Tees Reaction

Objectives:
- Shortens the swing
- Improves reaction time
- Improves hand-eye coordination and focus
- Teaches the hitter to hit outside and inside pitches
- Teaches the hitter to stay back

Degree of Difficulty: 2B

Equipment Needed:
- Two tees
- Baseballs
- Bat
- Partner
- Batting cage

Description: The hitter sets two tees with one of them simulating an inside pitch and the other simulating an outside pitch. A ball is set on each tee. The inside pitch is positioned in front of the plate in the direction of the inside corner. The outside tee is on the outside edge of the plate and is cutting the plate in half, front to back. The hitter takes his stance and waits for the command of a partner who will say either inside or outside, depending on which ball the partner wants the hitter to hit. The hitter reacts by pulling the ball if the command is to hit the ball on the inside tee and by hitting the ball the other way if the command is the outside tee.

Coaching Points:
- A ball has to be on each tee for every swing.
- The hitter needs to place the balls on the tee so that the two seams closest to him stand perpendicular to the ground The hitter then aims to hit the seam closest to him, allowing him to stay inside the ball on every swing.
- The hitter cannot hit the two balls during the swing. It can happen if the hitter goes around the ball and his swing is too long. Short, quick swings and staying inside the ball are the keys.
- The hitter should vary the height of the tees, so he does not groove his swing to one location.

Drill #49: Tee on a Bucket

Objectives:
- Shortens the swing
- Teaches the hitter to take the bat head right to the ball
- Makes the hitter to keep his hands up
- Improves arm extension

Degree of Difficulty:
- Dry swings: 2B
- Tee work: 2B
- Soft toss: 3B
- Flips: 3B
- Batting practice: 3B

Equipment Needed:
- Bucket or chair
- Tee
- Bat
- Baseballs
- Batting cage
- Optional: Partner

Description: The hitter begins by setting the bucket on the floor and placing the tee on top of the bucket. The tee's height must be set below where the hitter holds his hands after he has taken his stride. The hitter then stands in front of the bucket, with the tee parallel with his back shoulder. The idea is to swing the bat without hitting the tee (swing over the tee without hitting it). If the hitter hits the tee, the swing was long and/or he dropped his hands before starting the swing.

Coaching Points:
- The hitter should start this drill by doing dry swings. He should experiment with the height of the tee and his positioning. Then he can increase the degree of difficulty by moving up to soft tosses, flips, and batting practice.
- Repetition is the key. It develops muscle memory.
- The hitter needs to discipline his hands to stay up (above the ball).
- He should do 10 swings over the tee and then do five without it to program himself.
- During games and regular practice the hitter could visualize having the tee in front of and swing by trying not to hit it. This will help him keep the swing short.
- This drill also improves arm extension, because the hitter always hits the ball out in front. He gets immediate results and feedback.
- Using a tee as an obstacle is pretty safe, because if it is hit it just falls off the bucket. The hitter needs to use something that he will not be afraid to hit. Something harder or heavier might induce injury.

Drill #50: Drop Ball

Objectives:
- Shortens the swing
- Gives the hitter a one-motion swing
- Develops bat speed
- Improves reaction time
- Improves bat control
- Develops hand-eye coordination
- Disciplines the hitter to wait longer on off-speed pitches

Degree of Difficulty: 3B

Equipment Needed:
- Bat
- Baseballs
- Batting cage, hitting net, baseball field, or open space
- Partner

Description: The hitter stands at home plate as if he has already taken his stride. A partner stands at the other side of the plate. The partner holds a ball about eye level (higher for less-experienced hitters). The partner then drops the ball down on a straight line to the plate without letting the hitter know when he will let go of the ball. The hitter tries to find the ball as soon as possible and hit it before it hits the ground. The hitter needs to react quickly. This is what you call a "see the ball, hit the ball" drill.

Coaching Points:
- The partner should move the ball around so the hitter sees different pitch locations.
- The better the hitter becomes at performing this drill the lower the partner should hold the ball before he lets it go.
- The partner needs to stand at a distance at which he will not get hit either by the bat or a hit ball.
- The partner just needs to open his hand up and let go of the ball. He does not need to slam it down to make it go faster. The surprise drop is all the hitter needs to have a good workout.
- The hitter should always aim to hit the ball through the middle of the net.
- The hitter needs to be short and quick, but in control. As always, he just keeps his eyes on the contact area and try to see the ball hit the bat.

Drill #51: Net with a Tee

Objectives:
- Develops a shorter swing
- Develops good hitting mechanics
- Teaches the hitter to keep the hands inside the ball and hit through the ball

Degree of Difficulty: 3B

Equipment Needed:
- Tee
- Baseballs
- Bat
- Batting cage

Description: A tee is placed right next to the net in a location where the hitter can hit a ball positioned as if it was pitched down the middle of the plate. The idea is for the hitter to hit the ball on the tee without hitting the net. This drill is hard and gives the hitter instant feedback if the swing is too long. The hitter needs to try to hit the ball on a line drive. This will allow the hitter to develop a short swing and stay inside the ball. Pulling the ball might cause the hitter to roll over too soon and have a longer swing.

Coaching Points:
- This is a muscle memory drill, so repetition is the key.
- The instant feedback this drill provides is especially valuable if the hitter is working by himself.
- The hitter can follow the 10 + 5 routine.

Drill #52: Back Foot on a Block

Objectives:
- Eliminates uppercut
- Helps the hitter to take the bat head right to the ball
- Shortens the swing

Degree of Difficulty:
- Dry swings/tee work: 1B
- Soft tosses/flips: 2B

Equipment Needed:
- Concrete block
- Tennis or turf shoes
- Bat
- Baseballs
- Batting cage or hitting net
- Optional: Tee, screen, partner

Description: This drill should be done when wearing tennis or turf shoes. The hitter puts his back foot on top of a lying concrete block, which will automatically allow the back half of the body to be on top of the front half. Then, the hitter takes his swings. This position will make the hitter take the bat to the ball, thus shortening his swing. Remind the hitter that a long swing will make him inconsistent, so he should strive to develop the shortest path to the ball that he can.

Coaching Points:
- This drill is great for hitters who have an uppercut or want to work on being short to the ball.
- The hitter never wears spikes when doing this drill.
- This drill can be done during flips, soft toss, tee work, and dry swinging.
- Make sure the concrete block is strong enough to hold the hitter's weight.

Drill #53: Inside Tee the Other Way

Objectives:
- Teaches the hitter to stay inside the ball
- Shorten the swing
- Improves arm extension through the ball

Degree of Difficulty: 3B

Equipment Needed:
- Tee
- Bat
- Baseballs
- Hitting net or batting cage

Description: The hitter places the tee in an inside pitch location (e.g., inside corner, in front of the front foot). The hitter then tries to hit the ball on the tee to the opposite field. The hitter starts the tee around the inside corner of the plate, then moves it closer to him to make it more challenging. The hitter needs to get the hands out in front while keeping the bat head lagging back to hit the ball with the bat head. Remember, in a race between the hands and the barrel, the hands always win.

Coaching Point:
- The high and inside fastball is the toughest pitch to hit with authority. If the hitter can stay inside this pitch, all the other ones will be easier to hit.

Drill #54: Tee and Overhand Flip to the Screen

Objectives:
- Adds a sense of timing to tee work
- Improves swing mechanics

Degree of Difficulty: 2B

Equipment Needed:
- Tee
- Bat
- Baseballs
- Batting cage
- Screen
- Partner

Description: The hitter sets the tee as he normally would. The partner sets himself behind a screen about 15 feet away from the hitter in the direction of the pitcher with a ball in his throwing hand. The hitter gets ready to hit. The partner goes through his windup with the hitter looking at his motion. The hitter waits until the front leg is going down to start his separation (the hands go back as the front foot goes forward). The hitter lands the stride and quickly switches his focus from the pitcher to the ball on the tee and hits it right back to the screen.

Coaching Points:
- This drill not only makes tee work more fun, but also improves the hitter's concentration.
- The hitter needs to make sure not to keep his face to his partner, but instead bring the head down and keep it down during the swing (and keep looking at the tee after the ball is hit).

Drill #55: The Three Sound Swing

Objectives:
- Improves bat speed
- Makes the swing more compact
- Allows the hitter to be shorter and quicker to the ball

Degree of Difficulty:
- Dry swings: 1B
- Tee work, soft toss, flips: 2B
- Batting practice, machine: 3B

Equipment Needed:
- Bat
- Balls
- Batting cage or field
- Optional: punching bag

Description: The hitter does this drill by trying to listen in his head to the following three sounds at the same time:
- The chin hitting the back shoulder (imaginary sound)
- The ball hitting the bat (contact)
- The inside of the back knee hitting a punching bag between the legs (If a punching bag is not available, the hitter should imagine the sound.)

Of course, he will only hear one of those sounds (the ball hitting the bat), but by trying to listen to the three sounds, he will make his swing faster and shorter. To do this drill properly, the hands and the chin need to cross each other. As the hands are going forward, the head is going backward to meet the back shoulder half way.

Coaching Points:
- The hitter needs to put the word "fast" in his head and do this drill as quickly as he can.
- The hitter should try to hold his balance at the end of the swing. Holding like a statute for a count or two at the end of the swing will improve his balance.

Drill #56: Crossing the Head and Hands

Objectives:
- Teaches the hitter to use his hands properly
- Disciplines the head to stay down
- Improves rotation and power

Degree of Difficulty:
- Dry swings: 1B
- Tee work: 2B
- Soft toss/flips: 2B

Equipment Needed:
- Bat
- Balls
- Optional: Tee

Description: This is a simple but challenging drill in which the hitter tries to cross his hands and his head. What this means is that as the hands are going forward, the head goes back. The idea is to discipline the head not to fly out. The hitter needs to swing in a way in which the chin hits the back shoulder at the end of the swing. He must make sure that he does not turn his head sideways and turn the back ear to the ground, which gives a false sense of keeping the head down. For the hands to work properly, they need to go underneath the chin.

Coaching Point:
- A big reason why the head flies out is the hitter wants to see where he hits the ball. He needs to make sure that he has made contact before he raises his head to find the ball. He should rely on his first base coach for that.

Drill #57: The Dollar Bill Swing

Objectives:
- Improves swing path and extension
- Improves bat control
- Makes practice fun and more competitive

Degree of Difficulty:
- Tee work: HR
- Soft toss: HR
- Flips/batting practice: 3B

Equipment:
- Dollar bill
- Bat
- Balls
- Batting cage
- Coach or partner
- Optional: Tee

Description: The coach sets a dollar bill at different locations in the batting cage depending on what the hitter is working on. The dollar bill is hung through one of the holes in the net of the batting cage. The idea is for the hitter to try to hit the ball to the location around the dollar. If the dollar falls down, the dollar goes to the hitter. The first location should be straight away to the other end of the cage. As the hitter gets better, the dollar can be positioned so the hitter goes the other way or hits the ball to his pull side. This drill can be done at the end of the hitting session.

Coaching Points:
- Young players love this drill. They concentrate and work hard to get that dollar bill.
- The partner or coach needs to set up the bill so it is not easy for it to fall.

Drill #58: PVC Bat Speed

Objectives:
- Develops bat speed
- Teaches the hitter to accelerate through the swing
- Teaches the hitter where in his swing he develops the most bat speed

Degree of Difficulty: 2B

Equipment Needed:
- One-inch-thick PVC at least as long as a bat (tape can be added to simulate a handle)
- Open space
- Optional: Baseballs, bat, batting cage, tee, tape

Description: The goal of this drill is for the hitter to swing the pipe as fast as he can on every swing, paying attention to the loud sound of the swing cutting through the air. He needs to hear the pipe accelerating through the zone and he should compete with himself or a partner to see who makes the loudest sound or swings fastest. The hitter needs to challenge himself to swing faster with each swing. As soon as he notices his bat speed decreasing, he should stop and take a little breather. After he has gathered some energy, he should do another set.

Coaching Points:
- The hitter can do a set with the pipe and then a set of five reps with his regular bat to transfer the overspeed feeling of the drill to his swing. Another option is to have him perform a program of three or four sets with the pipe and then take his normal swing with his bat. He can also add a heavy bat to the mix and do an overload/overspeed workout.
- The hitter should tape one end of the bat as a bat grip and/or use batting gloves so the pipe does not slip. If the hitter has extra tape, he can tape around the end of the pipe to resemble a knob of a bat. This is the safest option, as the pipe will not fly out of his hands even when he swings his hardest.
- Make sure that the pipe is not too thick for the hitter's hands. The hitter will also need to find a thickness that resembles the handle of his bat.

Drill #59: Blowing the Hands Away

Objectives:
- Helps the hitter to throw his hands out in front
- Develops a tension-free swing
- Makes the hitter swing faster
- Helps the hitter gather his power before the swing

Degree of Difficulty:
- Dry swings: 2B
- Tee work: 2B
- Soft toss: 3B
- Flips: 3B
- Batting practice: HR

Equipment Needed:
- Bat
- Baseballs
- Batting cage or open space
- Optional: Tee

Description: To do this drill, the hitter smoothly and slowly takes a deep breath while he is taking his hands back. After he lands his stride he holds his breath during the separation of the stride and the swing (at the launching position). As he starts his swing, the hitter explosively breathes out, simulating blowing his hands away from himself.

Coaching Points:
- By blowing his hands away, the hitter will accomplish a few important things: he will be able to release his power, relax, and get rid of stored tension. Every time a hitter looks rigid or tense during a swing he is likely holding his breath. Have the hitter imagine a weight lifter doing 10 repetitions with one single breath or a sprinter running 100 yards without recovering any oxygen. They would look tense and their faces would be all red.
- As a rule of thumb, a person needs to inhale to gather strength and exhale during the more difficult part of the exercise.
- Breathing will also help the hitter slow down in their approach to the ball. This is an important tip for hitters who jump to the ball, or commit too soon.
- The hitter should start blowing his hands away from the beginning of the swing. This will allow him to have a tension-free swing from beginning to end.
- The first few times he tries this breathing pattern the hitter might feel a little lightheaded because of the deep breathing. Allow him to take any needed breaks, but advise him to keep working on it and it will eventually become second nature to him.

Drill #60: Back Knee on the Ground

Objectives:
- Isolates the upper body
- Teaches the proper use of the hands and arms during the swing
- Isolates the head and increases head control

Degree of Difficulty:
- Dry swings: 1B
- Tee work: 1B
- Soft toss: 2B
- Flips: 2B

Equipment Needed:
- Bat
- Baseballs
- Batting cage or hitting net
- Optional: Tee, partner, screen

Description: The basic idea of this drill is to work on the upper body during the swing. By putting the back knee on the ground, the hitter isolates the upper body, ensuring a better use of his hands and arms. This teaches the upper body what to do, without the bottom half getting in the way. The hitter can position himself in one of two ways:

- The hitter puts his back knee on the ground and the front foot flat on the ground and the front knee bent at a 45-degree angle.
- The hitter puts his back knee on the ground, but with the front leg straight, pointing to the pitcher's mound with only the inside of the front foot on the ground.

After choosing which position is better suited for him, the hitter then takes his swings, finishing them with a proper follow-through.

Coaching Points:
- The hitter should emphasize throwing his hands to the ball and staying inside the ball.
- The hitter needs to keep his head down throughout the swing for a short and compact swing.
- Remind the hitter to pay attention to the all upper-body hitting mechanics.
- If the hitter decides to use the second position, he needs to make sure that he stays inside the ball and hits the ball the other way. If he rolls over or pulls it too much he could hit his front foot.

Drill #61: Towel Bat I

Objectives:
- Teaches hitter the inside out swing
- Improves wrist action (snap)

Degree of Difficulty: 2B

Equipment Needed:
- Medium-sized towel
- Old wooden bat, nails, and a hammer (or an aluminum bat and tape)

Description: The hitter prepares for this drill by putting the towel on the head of the bat as follows:
- Aluminum: Tape the towel to the top of the barrel. Make sure that it is tight enough that it won't slide off when the hitter is swinging hard.
- Wood: Nail the towel around the top of the barrel. Leave about two-thirds of the towel off the bat.

The hitter dry-swings as if he has a whip in his hand, trying to get the towel to make a snapping sound. The louder the sound, the better contact will be.

Coaching Points:
- Where the hitter hears the sound is important. The snap should be heard where contact is expected, which is where the hitter needs to generate the most bat speed.
- The hitter needs to use his hands properly for this drill to work. When a swing is short and quick, he won't hear the towel make as much of a "swish" noise from the beginning of the swing to contact. Instead, he just tries to snap it in front and follow through.
- The hitter should repeat the swing as many times as possible, trying to snap the towel louder with each subsequent swing. This is a muscle memory drill, so repetition is the key.
- The hitter must not use the towel bat as a toy or as a weapon to hit his friends. It could be dangerous to play with it. He needs to make sure there is nobody around when he is working with it.

Drill #62: One-Arm Toss to a Net

Objectives:
- Improves the beginning of the swing
- Teaches the hitter to throw his hands to the ball
- Improves arm extension on contact
- Simulates the swing and improves bat speed

Degree of Difficulty: 2B

Equipment Needed:
- Ball (or a bucket of balls)
- Batting cage or hitting net

Description: The hitter holds a baseball with his bottom hand and sets up in his launching position. The other arm should be behind the back. The hitter must flex his front elbow as much as he can (so it resembles a "V"). The hitter then "throws" the ball forward by extending the elbow and raising the arm about shoulder high. He should do it as fast as he can and not roll the hand over (i.e., the palm stays facing down).

To work the top hand, the hitter holds the ball with the top hand and sets the other one behind the back.

The hitter then takes the hand to its launching position. The hitter must bring the elbow in front of the body before he lets go off the ball. The arm is flexed and when it cannot go forward anymore the hitter extends the arm and tosses the ball. The top hand finishes with the palm.

Coaching Points:
- The throws should be made by extending the elbows only.
- The hitter should toss the ball into the net as hard as possible
- Remember, this drill starts at the launching position and requires only one movement: taking the hand down and forward (i.e., extending the elbow).
- The hitter should visualize that he is hitting different pitch locations.
- The hitter should do this drill at his convenience and when he is practicing by himself.
- The hitter must warm up his arms before doing this drill.

Drill #63: Tee Work Adjustment

Objectives:
- Prevents the hitter from grooving his swing to one location
- Lets hitter work on different pitch locations
- Improves hitting mechanics to all fields

Degree of Difficulty: 2B

Equipment Needed:
- Tee
- Bat and baseballs

Description: In this drill, the hitter simply takes batting practice while moving the tee to different locations and heights, thereby avoiding the common trap of taking 25 or 50 swings with the tee in a single spot.

Coaching Points:
- Tees are available that have different holes on the base so the hitter can change the position of the "pitch." If the hitter is using a standard tee that has only one position on the base, he should move the tee around to practice outside, inside, high, and low pitches.
- Remind the hitter to hit through the ball and take the bat head right to the ball. These are the keys of being successful with a high pitch.
- The hitter should make sure that he keeps his head down on contact.
- The hitter needs to stay inside the ball. If he needs a visual of where to hit the ball, he can place the ball on the tee with the two seams closest to himself standing perpendicular to the ground and then aim for the closest seam.

Drill #64: Dry Swings in Front of a Mirror

Objectives:
- Lets the hitter coach himself and see what he is doing when he swings
- Improves hitting mechanics

Degree of Difficulty: 2B

Equipment Needed:
- Bat
- Mirror

Description: The hitter sets himself in front of the mirror and dry swings his bat. He should go through his whole hitting process, checking to see how everything is working, from his stride to his follow-through. The hitter can set up in front of the mirror in one of two ways:
- The hitter faces the mirror as if the mirror is the pitcher. In this position the hitter will not be able to use his head properly, but he will be able to check his stride, alignment, the firmness of his front leg, balance, shoulder levelness, arm extension, etc.
- The mirror is located on the other side of the plate from the hitter. This is the best view for a hitter to see himself swinging a bat because the hitter can see his whole swing. The hitter needs to check every part of the swing to see what he is doing and what corrections are needed.

The hitter should experiment with his stance, stride, swing, and follow-through. He can see, for example, how his swing looks if he raises his hands or how his body reacts when he uses a higher kick.

Because he can see himself in the mirror, the hitter can decide if changing a part or parts of his swing might improve it.

A variation of this drill is using tape in the mirror. For this drill, the hitter places a long piece of white tape (a little longer than shoulder width) on a mirror at the height of his shoulders during his stance (he can use the help of a partner to do this). The hitter then sets up by facing the mirror and does the following:
- Gets in his stance and checks his shoulder alignment, making any necessary adjustments.
- Takes his stride without looking at the mirror, instead looking to where a pitcher would be. After the hitter lands the stride and is in his launching position, he looks at the tape checks his shoulder alignment at this phase of the swing. He then makes any needed adjustments.
- Takes his swing while looking down to where a ball would be in the contact area. After finishing the swing, the hitter looks at the mirror to see if the shoulders are aligned correctly.

Coaching Points:
- Teach the hitter to look for the collapse of the back shoulder, whether he has risen up or gone down during the swing, and whether the front shoulder is open prematurely.
- The hitter needs to find as big a mirror as possible, like those in a weight room.
- Remind the hitter to make sure that there is enough distance before he starts swinging.

Drill #65: Super Slow Motion Dry Swings

Objectives:
- Improves concentration
- Increases body awareness
- Allows hitters to work on their own

Degree of Difficulty: 2B

Equipment Needed:
- Bat
- Open space
- Optional: Heavy doughnut or ankle weight

Description: In this drill, the hitter performs his swing in super slow motion. He should move his bat an inch or so per second. He can eventually progress to even slower speeds. The hitter can also hold for five seconds, and then keep going.

Coaching Points:
- When swinging at regular speed, a hitter does not need to concentrate as much. But slowing the swing down requires extreme concentration and will involve the whole body. The hitter will be sweating and shaking after a few repetitions.
- This drill can also help the hitter become aware of any bad habits he might have, especially at the beginning of the swing.
- To make this drill more challenging, slow it down or use a heavier bat (or add the doughnut or ankle weight to the hitter's bat).

Drill #66: Tee Work with a Target on the Net

Objectives:
- Improves bat control
- Improves hand-eye coordination
- Improves focus and concentration
- Teaches proper swinging mechanics

Degree of Difficulty: 3B

Equipment Needed:
- Tee
- Hitting net or batting cage
- Baseballs
- Bat
- Towel

Description: The hitter either sets up in a batting cage or sets the tee in front of a net approximating the length of the batting cage. The partner then places a target in different parts of the net or batting cage (like a hung towel). The hitter then tries to hit the target to improve his hand-eye coordination and bat control. The feeder can leave the target at the same place for a round and then switch it or he can move the hitter around the plate and leave the target at the same place. By moving the around, the hitter will be to go the other way or pull the ball while keeping his balance and developing bat control.

Coaching Points:
- The feeder should not use chairs or something similar as targets because they make a lot of noise if the ball hits them.
- The hitter needs to place the balls on the tee so that the two seams closest to him stand perpendicular to the ground. The hitter then tries to hit the seam closest to him so he can stay inside the ball and shorten his swing.

Drill #67: Backward Chaining

Objectives:
- Teaches the hitter to become his own coach
- Forces the hitter to swing the bat properly

Degree of Difficulty:
- Tee drill/dry swings: 2B
- Soft toss/flips/batting practice: 3B

Equipment Needed:
- Bat
- Baseballs
- Batting cage or baseball field

Description: With this drill, the hitter aims to make corrections to his swing by starting from the end of his swing and working backward. The hitter starts with a perfect follow-through and then goes to his stance. The hitter then swings the bat, trying to reach that perfect follow-through position of front foot closed, back foot's shoelaces pointing to the pitcher, bat behind the head, hands over the front shoulder, and the face pointing to the contact position. When the hitter is aware of his final destination he usually does what is necessary to get there.

Coaching Points:
- This is a good drill to have hitters perform in front of a mirror.
- At the end of each swing, have the hitter stop at his follow-through and check if he reached the position he wanted.

Drill #68: No-Stride Ankle Weight

Objectives:
- Improves the use of the hands
- Quiets "happy feet"
- Helps the hitter generate maximum power
- Eliminates wasted motion

Degree of Difficulty:
- Dry swings/tee work: 1B
- Soft toss/flips: 2B
- Batting practice/machine: 3B

Equipment Needed:
- Two ankle weights (the heavier the better)
- Bat
- Baseballs
- Optional: Partner, tee

Description: The hitter tightens the weights around his ankles and tries to swing the bat as he normally does. The weight will force him to keep his feet in place, giving him instant feedback about how and to where he has been moving his feet. This is a good drill for hitters who have "happy feet" (i.e., those who move their feet too much), because it will teach the hitter to stay in place during the swing.

Coaching Point:
- After the hitter gets used to using his arms properly, he can incorporate a back foot pivot.

Drill #69: Catch the Ball with Two Hands

Objectives:
- Improves the way the hitter uses his hands during the swing
- Improves the swing path
- Improves hand-eye coordination and ball tracking

Degree of Difficulty: 2B

Equipment Needed:
- Baseballs
- Partner
- Open space

Description: The partner sets up in a soft toss position and the hitter sets up at home plate without a bat but with the hands in the hitting position. The partner tosses the ball to the hitting area and the hitter tries to catch it with both hands (sandwiching it) and hold for balance.

Coaching Points:
- This drill will teach the hitter to hit the ball as he is turning, to use his hands as a unit, and to improve hand-eye and body coordination.
- To make this drill more challenging, the hitter can wear wrist weights or close one eye.
- The hitter needs to make sure that the back shoulder hits the chin at the end of the swing.

Drill #70: Flat Bat

Objectives:
- Improves contact
- Improves palm-up, palm-down position of the hands on contact

Degree of Difficulty: 2B

Equipment Needed:
- Tennis racket
- Bat
- Tape
- Tennis balls
- Partner

Description: To prepare for this drill, the hitter tapes the racket handle to the bat head (turning the bat into a makeshift flat bat). A partner then tosses tennis balls to the hitter and the hitter tries to hit the ball with the flat side of the racket. After a set of 10 repetitions, the hitter can use another bat to transfer the feeling of this drill to his regular swing.

Coaching Point:
- The hitter should try to see the ball hit the bat during this drill, as this will help him make better contact.

Drill #71: Arm Extension

Objectives:
- Develops power
- Develops bat speed
- Improves arm extension on contact
- Develops hand-eye coordination and bat control
- Teaches the hitter to take the bat head right to the ball (shortens the swing)

Degree of Difficulty:
- Tee work: 2B
- Soft toss: 2B
- Flips: 3B
- Batting practice: 3B

Equipment Needed:
- Bat
- Baseballs
- Batting glove
- Batting cage, hitting net, baseball field, or open space
- Optional: Tee

Description: The hitter places a batting glove or his hat about five feet in front of home plate (between himself and the pitcher). The hitter takes five swings, aiming to hit the object he placed in front of him. The partner then moves the object to about 10 feet away and again the hitter aims to hit it with five swings of the bat. The object is then moved to about 15 feet away and the hitter again takes five more swings. The hitter then finishes the drill by taking five swings without the object in place.

Coaching Points:
- Problems with arm extension usually manifest in one of three ways: the hitter only seems to have solid contact to the opposite field, he cannot pull the ball with authority, and he is getting jammed often.
- Point out to the hitter that as the object moves farther from the plate his extension improves and contact becomes more solid.
- The hitter should aim to hit the object, but make sure his body stays back. In other words, just because he is trying to hit the object does not mean he should jump toward it. Remind him, "hands in front, body back".
- After he masters hitting the object as it is moved forward on a straight line to the pitcher, the hitter should move the object around to the right and left sides. This will teach him to extend his arms when he is pulling the ball and when he is hitting the ball the other way.
- To hit the ball to his pull side, the hitter must remember that he needs to hit the ball out in front of the plate. To hit the ball the other way, he must wait a little longer.
- This is a muscle memory drill. Repetition is the key.

Drill #72: Two-Tee Practice

Objectives:
- Teaches the hitter to stay through the ball
- Makes the swing more level
- Improves arm extension

Degree of Difficulty: 2B

Equipment Needed:
- Two tees
- Bat
- Baseballs
- Batting cage or hitting net

Description: The hitter sets the tees one in front of the other about 10 to 15 inches apart with the one closer to him placed where he normally sets it when he is just using one tee. The hitter puts a ball on each tee with the height being the same for both tees. The idea is to hit both balls by swinging through them and making sure that the ball on the second tee goes right to the middle of the net or to the opposite field. The hitter needs to concentrate on keeping himself down and not cutting his swing short by going around the ball.

Coaching Points:
- This drill will teach the hitter how to be short to the ball and long on the extension.
- The hitter should perform this drill often if he has trouble staying through the ball.
- The back elbow should be bent on contact (of the first ball), and the hitter should forcefully push the ball away as he is extending that arm.

Drill #73: Top Hand to the Pitcher

Objectives:
- Improves arm extension
- Teaches the hitter to hit through the ball
- Enhances contact by making the hitter hit the ball more solidly

Degree of Difficulty:
- Dry swings/tee work: 2B
- Soft tosses/flips: 3B
- Batting practice: 3B

Equipment Needed:
- Baseballs
- Bat
- Feeder
- Batting cage or baseball field
- Screen
- Optional: Tee

Description: The hitter takes his stance at home plate. He then goes through his normal swing, but right after contact lets the top hand come off the bat as if he were reaching for the pitcher. In other words, the hitter swings the bat, hits the ball with both hands on the bat, and then lets the top hand go off the bat. He points his fingers to the pitcher with the palm facing down and the arm extended. He also must push the back shoulder in the same direction of the hand and keep his head down. This will force the hitter to stay through the ball by hitting the ball with both hands and maintaining good balance throughout the swing.

Coaching Points:
- If a hitter chooses to let go of the top hand during his swing, this drill will teach him to do so properly while allowing for solid contact.
- The hitter needs to remember to push forward after contact. He should not move forward before he starts his swing (i.e., drift), but instead as he is hitting the ball (i.e., weight shift).
- The hitter might want to experiment with this approach as his normal swing. It will keep him balanced and help him hit through the ball, plus it is very simple to do.

Drill #74: Statue

Objectives:
- Improves balance at the end of the swing
- Makes the swing more efficient

Degree of Difficulty:
- Dry swings/tee work: 1B
- Soft toss/flips: 2B
- Batting practice/machine: 3B

Equipment Needed:
- Bat
- Baseballs
- Batting cage or open space

Description: In this drill the hitter swings the bat as he normally would, but at the end of his swing he freezes like a statue for at least a count of three. The hitter holds his balance as if someone is going to take a picture for his baseball card at the end of the swing. If he is shaking or moving all over the place the hitter is not transferring his weight or rotating properly.

Coaching Points:
- If the hitter is falling away from the plate, he might be spinning, or moving both feet in the same direction at the same time.
- If the hitter is falling back, he might not be transferring his weight properly.
- If the hitter is falling to the plate, he might be diving, or striding or stepping toward home plate.
- If the hitter is going forward to the pitcher, he might be drifting—taking his step toward the pitcher and swinging the bat while moving sideways—or lunging—stepping or striding without firming up the front leg.
- If the hitter is shaking, he might have weak legs and a program to strengthen them should be started.
- The hitter might feel some soreness after doing this drill at the inner and outer thighs and at the calves. These are the stabilizing balance muscles of the legs. If they are sore, that simply means that the hitter is exercising those muscles and should not get discouraged.

Hold for three seconds

Drill #75: Look Back

Objectives:
- Teaches the hitter to finish his swing
- Forces the hitter to accelerate through the ball
- Improves rotational power and balance at the end of the swing

Degree of Difficulty:
- Dry swings/tee work: 1B
- Soft toss/flips: 2B
- Batting practice/machine: 3B

Equipment Needed:
- Bat
- Baseballs
- Partner
- Batting cage

Description: In this drill the hitter forgets about hitting the ball and concentrates on finishing his swing. The hitter swings the bat by taking the bat all the way back so that if he looks back toward the direction of the catcher he is able to see the bat head. The hitter needs to make sure to accelerate through the ball. The key is that the hitter does not stop the swing when he makes contact, but instead keeps pushing through without a pause during the swing.

Coaching Point:
- This drill forces the hitter to keep his balance at the end of the swing, which will make the swing more efficient and generate more bat speed.

6

Drills to Improve Rotation and Leg Use During the Swing

Drill #76: Stop Stepping in the Bucket

Objective:
• Stops the hitter from stepping away from the plate

Degree of Difficulty:
• Dry swings: 1B
• Tee work: 1B
• Soft tosses: 2B
• Flips: 2B

Equipment Needed:
• Sand back, concrete block, or old tire
• Bat
• Baseballs
• Batting cage

Description: The hitter stands at the plate as he normally would, and places an object (sand back, concrete block, or old tire) behind his front foot heel. The hitter then steps as he normally does. If he steps out, the object will stop him and give him instant feedback about how he is striding.

Coaching Point:
• The hitter needs to try to stride square to the pitcher so he can see the ball better and generate more power.

Drill #77: Lazy Susan

Objectives:
- Improves the rotation of the back foot and leg
- Develops power

Degree of Difficulty:
- Dry swings/tee work: 1B
- Soft toss/flips: 2B
- Batting practice: 2B

Equipment Needed:
- Lazy Susan (4″ x 4″ rotating bearing that can be purchased at most hardware stores)
- Bat
- Baseballs
- Tee
- Batting cage

Description: The hitter places the Lazy Susan under the ball of his back foot and lets the bearings help him pivot the back leg properly. The hitter pivots the back leg by taking the back heel back in the direction of the catcher and finishing the pivot on the big toe.

Coaching Points:
- The hitter needs to make sure that he uses a surface that does not allow the Lazy Susan to slip.
- Putting pressure on the Lazy Susan helps the hitter pivot more effectively.

Drill #78: Squish the Bug

Objectives:
- Improves the back foot's pivot
- Improves the use of the legs during the swing
- Develops explosiveness

Degree of Difficulty:
- Dry swings: 2B
- Tee work: 2B
- Soft toss: 2B
- Flips: 3B
- Batting practice: 3B

Equipment Needed:
- Bat
- Baseballs
- A piece of paper
- Batting cage, hitting net
- Tennis shoes
- Optional: Tee, partner

Description: The hitter gets a piece of paper and forms a ball with it. He then puts the paper under the ball of his back foot, making sure the paper is big enough that he will feel it. The hitter then goes through his hitting process, pivoting on top of the paper as if he is squishing a bug. As the hitter gets better, he places the ball of paper under the big toe. This is how he should pivot the back foot.

Coaching Points:
- Most of a hitter's power comes from his legs, his "core" area (abs, lower back, buttocks, thighs), and from the proper use of those muscles during the back foot pivot. If the hitter cannot execute that action correctly he will be an upper-body hitter and only utilize one-third of his total power source. This drill can remedy that problem.
- A lot of coaches use the expression "squish the bug," but many hitters cannot seem to grasp the idea because they have a hard time visualizing how to do the action. Having the paper underneath his shoe will give a hitter something concrete that he can feel.
- If done properly, this drill has the potential to help the hitter get rid of bad hitting habits such as drifting and rising up before contact, while teaching the right way to use the back leg. This drill is especially effective with younger hitters.
- Make sure that the hitter is not falling back when the paper is under the ball of the foot. If he is, the ball of paper needs to be placed under the big toe instead.
- This is a muscle memory drill, so repetition is the key.
- For proper leg use, the front leg has to be as firm as a rock and the back leg must form an "L" shape at the end of the swing.
- The hitter needs to do this drill on a flat, hard surface and while wearing tennis shoes.
- The hitter needs to start doing this drill with dry swings, later moving on to more difficult hitting practice.

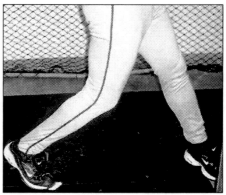

Drill #79: Sand Bag Back Foot Pivot

Objective:
• Teaches the hitter how to pivot the back foot properly

Degree of Difficulty:
• Dry swings: 1B
• Tee work/soft toss: 2B
• Flips/batting practice: 3B

Equipment Needed:
• Sand bag or similar object
• Bat
• Baseballs
• Tee
• Partner

Description: The hitter sets a sand bag behind the toes of the back foot. The hitter then swings the bat while trying to hit the sand bag with the outside of his foot. The hitter pivots on the big toe, powerfully and cleanly hitting the bag.

Coaching Point:
• Most of a hitter's power comes from the rotation of the body through the ball, so a proper back leg pivot is essential to developing great bat speed during the swing.

Drill #80: Sand Bags Inside the Feet

Objectives:
- Teaches the hitter how to use his legs properly
- Improves power

Degree of Difficulty:
- Dry swings: 1B
- Tee work/soft toss: 2B
- Flips/batting practice: 3B

Equipment Needed:
- Two sand bags or one tire
- Bat
- Baseballs
- Partner
- Batting cage or baseball field

Description: The hitter performs this drill from his launching position (having already taken his stride). The hitter sets one of the sand bags inside the front foot and the other inside the back foot (or sets a tire between his feet). The hitter then swings the bat, making sure that the feet stay outside the shoulders and the upper body stays inside the knees.

Coaching Point:
- To properly use his power, the hitter needs to keep his feet apart during his swing. If the back foot goes toward the front foot, the hitter's eye level will rise, making timing more difficult. If the hitter tends to lift the back foot off the ground, he should work on trying to lift the back foot backward instead of forward.

Drill #81: Hitting on a Balance Beam

Objectives:
- Improves balance
- Improves softness, or the ability to land the stride softly and maintain focus and control
- Provides upper-body swing practice

Degree of Difficulty:
- Dry swings: 3B
- Tee work: 3B
- Soft toss: HR
- Flips: HR
- Batting practice: GS

Equipment Needed:
- Beam (4" x 4" by 4' long; can be purchased at most hardware stores)
- Bat
- Baseballs
- Batting cage or hitting net
- Tennis shoes
- Optional: Tee

Description: The key to this drill is to be able to swing the bat on the beam without falling off before, during, or after the swing. The hitter starts by taking dry swings and progresses to a more challenging hitting practice. The hitter can follow this routine:

- Take the stride
- Take the stride with the eyes closed
- Take dry swings with and without the eyes closed
- Tee work
- Soft tosses
- Flips
- Batting practice

Coaching Points:
- The hitter should shoot for 10 swings in a row without falling off. The hitter should do these drills as often as possible to improve his balance.
- Balance is a skill that can be improved with practice. Incorporate a balance program into team workouts at least twice a week.
- Remind hitters to always take his stride and land softly.
- Great hitters have a lot of things in common, and great balance is one of them.
- This drill should only be performed while wearing tennis shoes with good traction.
- When first doing this drill, the hitter's inner thighs will get sore. Do not allow him to get discouraged and remind him that this is a sign that he is exercising muscles he may have neglected in the past.
- Set the beam in a dry, safe place. Falling off the beam is easy to do, so take the necessary precautions.

Drill #82: Tire Behind the Heel

Objectives:
- Improves back foot pivot and rotation
- Improves power

Degree of Difficulty:
- Dry swings/tee work: 1B
- Soft toss/flips: 2B

Equipment Needed:
- Bat
- Baseballs
- Tire
- Batting cage
- Partner

Description: The hitter sets an old tire next to the outside of his back foot. The hitter then swings by trying to push the tire as far back as possible. The hitter tries to swing in a coordinated way so that the hands start as he is pushing the tire back. This drill can be done in two ways:
- The hitter stays at home plate and brings the tire back to the starting position after each swing.
- The hitter stays between the screen and home plate. The feeder starts a little farther behind the screen than he normally would. The feeder tosses the ball and the hitter swings, but instead of moving the tire back to the starting position and returning to home plate, the hitter moves next to the tire and performs as many repetition as space allows. This version of the drill will improve depth perception because of the continuous change of distance.

Coaching Points:
- The hitter should not use a tire that is so heavy that he would not be able to move it during the swing.
- The idea is to make the hitter feel that as the hands are going forward, the back foot goes back.

Drill #83: Bat Behind the Back Rotation

Objectives:
- Improves rotational power
- Teaches the hitter to use his legs properly
- Improves hand-eye coordination
- Improves power and bat speed

Degree of Difficulty: 3B

Equipment Needed:
- Bat
- Baseballs
- Batting cage
- Partner

Description: The hitter places his bat behind his back as some players do when working on hip rotation or warming up. The hitter stands at home plate, and waits for the partner to underhand a flip right on top of the plate. The hitter then tries to hit the ball right back up the middle with the part of the bat that is exposed. After every 10 repetitions, the hitter takes five or 10 swings with a pitched ball.

Coaching Points:
- A longer bat, a light barbell, or any similar object can be used.
- The hitter should never do this drill with batting practice or overhand flips. Only underhand flips from a partner who has good control is recommended.
- The hitter should not try to hit the ball to his pull side because often such hits are caused by going around the ball. Instead, he should hit the ball right back to the middle.
- The hitter should turn powerfully to hit the ball as hard as possible.

Drill #84: Chin Shoulder-to-Shoulder

Objectives:
- Improves balance
- Gives the hitter a tighter rotation
- Improves the ability to see the ball
- Helps the hitter keep the front side closed

Degree of Difficulty:
- Dry swings/tee work: 1B
- Soft tosses/flips: 2B
- Batting practice: 3B

Equipment Needed:
- Baseballs
- Bat
- Batting cage or baseball field
- Optional: Tee, partner, screen

Description: The hitter takes his stance at home plate with his chin on the front shoulder. The hitter then starts the downward path of the swing with his hands. The eyes track the ball all the way to the contact area. The back shoulder finishes the body's rotation and meets the chin to complete the swing and the follow-through.

Coaching Points:
- Moving the chin from shoulder to shoulder gives the hitter a more balanced swing and a tighter rotation for more power. When the back shoulder does not touch the chin, the head leaves the contact area, the head flies over the front shoulder, the ball seems to disappear from the hitter, the swing is longer, and the end of the swing tends to be off balance.
- The body follows the head, so if the hitter keeps his head down the swing will be down and short. On the other hand, if the head flies out the swing will be longer and contact will not be as consistent. If the head is down on contact, the body will be balanced and maximum power can be executed.
- By having the chin on the shoulder, the hitter accomplishes three things:
  ✓ The chin stops the front shoulder from turning inward too much and from opening up too soon.
  ✓ The front shoulder stops the head from flying out.
  ✓ The hitter is able to see the pitcher with both eyes and the shoulders will be square.
- The hitter should not see where the ball goes after he hits it. He needs to keep his head down. The first base coach will help the hitter find the ball as he is hustling to first base.
- Some hitters that keep the top hand on the bat have a hard time getting the back shoulder to touch the chin.
- You might discover that if the hitter lets go of the top hand right after hitting the ball, the hitter can keep his head down better and the shoulder touches the chin. Hitters and coaches should experiment to see what approach is best for a particular hitter.
- Some hitters start with the chin off the front shoulder, but when they take their hands back they make sure that the chin is on the front shoulder. This is another approach a hitter can use to ensure proper head use.

7

Drills to Develop Bat Speed and Improve Reaction

Drill #85: Hitting with a Lighter Bat or Fungo

Objectives:
- Develops bat speed
- Develops explosiveness

Degree of Difficulty:
- Dry swings: 1B
- Tee work: 1B
- Soft toss: 2B
- Flips: 2B
- Batting practice: 2B

Equipment Needed:
- The hitter's regular bat
- A lighter bat or fungo
- Baseballs
- Batting cage, hitting net, baseball field, or open space
- Partner
- Optional: Tee

Description: This drill will overspeed the hitter's swing, and it is up to the hitter to challenge himself to swing faster than he normally does. This drill can be done with either a lighter bat or a fungo.

- Lighter bat: Ideally, the hitter should use a bat about five to eight ounces lighter than his normal bat, but can use whatever bat is available. This is a good drill no matter how light the bat is.
- Fungo: A fungo is lighter and a lot weaker than a regular bat. If a wooden fungo is used for this drill, the hitter should only perform dry swings; tee work and soft tosses can also be performed, but a pitched ball might break the fungo. An aluminum fungo is a lot stronger and might withstand the pounding of a pitched ball or flips. Make sure that the fungo used is strong enough to endure the practice the hitter wants to do.

Coaching Points:
- After every 10 swings with the lighter bat, the hitter should swing his regular bat at least five times while trying to swing his bat as fast as he was swinging the lighter one. Three to four sets every other day should be enough.
- The hitter should compete with himself, always trying to swing faster than his previous swing. When he feels that his bat speed is dramatically slowing down, end the drill.

Drill #86: Flips Coming from Behind

Objectives:
- Improves bat speed
- Improves reaction time
- Improves bat control and arm extension
- Disciplines the hitter to wait back
- Improves hand-eye coordination

Degree of Difficulty: 3B

Equipment Needed:
- Bat
- Baseball
- Partner
- Batting cage

Description: For this drill, the hitter and flipper switch positions. The flipper gets behind the hitter, about 15 feet away (behind where the home plate umpire would be in a game). The flipper tosses the ball over the plate. The hitter finds the ball and tries to hit a line drive to the other side of the cage. This drill can be performed at three different levels of difficulty:
- The hitter takes his normal stance, but turns his head to the flipper, seeing the ball all the way.
- The hitter takes his normal stance, but this time he is looking straight ahead to the side of the cage.
- The hitter takes his normal stance, looking to where a pitcher would normally be. The hitter can't see the ball until it is in front of him. At this level, the flipper needs to say "ball" when he is letting go of the ball.

Coaching Points:
- The flipper must have good control to avoid hitting the hitter and toss strikes.
- This drill requires a lot of effort and the hitter needs to make sure that he has warmed up well before performing this drill.

Drill #87: Rapid Fire Flips without Legs

Objectives:
- Improves arm use and bat speed
- Conditions the hitter to last longer during the season
- Improves hand-eye coordination and bat control

Degree of Difficulty: HR

Equipment Needed:
- Bat
- Baseballs
- Partner
- Batting cage

Description: The hitter stands at the plate in a flip position. The partner tosses five to 10 balls to the hitter (depending on the hitter's conditioning level) one after the other without giving the hitter a break. The hitter swings the bat only using his arms, without pivoting or taking a stride. The fact that the hitter is only using his arms gives him an amazing workout while improving hand speed, reaction time, and hand-eye coordination.

Coaching Points:
- The hitter needs to make sure to warm up properly before doing this drill.
- If the hitter is doing this drill for conditioning purposes, this drill should be done at the end of practice. If the goal is instead on improving arm speed, the drill should be done at the beginning of practice.

Drill #88: Hard Underhand Flips

Objectives:
- Improves bat speed
- Improves reaction time
- Improves hand-eye coordination

Degree of Difficulty: 3B

Equipment Needed:
- Bat
- Baseballs
- Partner
- Batting cage

Description:The tosser tries to blow the ball by the hitter using an underhand, almost softball-like, motion. The hitter has to react quickly and try to hit the ball right back to the net, so the tosser needs to get his arm out of the way quickly. After a few repetitions, the tosser can tell the hitter that he will mix in some other types of flips (e.g., spinners, regular).

Coaching Point:
- The tosser can increase the degree of difficulty by either throwing harder or by throwing the pitches more inside. A heavier bat can also be used to increase workload.

Drill #89: Soft Toss—Two Balls at Once

Objectives:
• Develops bat speed
• Improves reaction time
• Improves bat control
• Develops hand-eye coordination
• Disciplines the hitter to wait back

Degree of Difficulty:
• Soft toss: 3B
• Flips: 3B

Equipment Needed:
• Bat
• Baseballs
• Batting cage, hitting net
• Partner

Description: The feeder holds two balls on his tossing hand and then tosses both of them at the same time, trying to toss one of them higher than the other one. After he lets go of the balls, he then shouts either "high" or "low," to let the hitter know which of the balls to hit.

Coaching Points:
• The feeder should hold the balls with the thumb pointing up to the sky, instead of to the side, because it is easier this way to toss one of the balls higher than the other one.
• The feeder holds the key to how challenging this drill is—to make it easier he shouts earlier and to make it tougher he waits longer.
• This drill will help the hitter wait longer on the ball and improve his reaction time. This is a very challenging but fun drill, which the hitters will enjoy.
• As a precaution, the feeder should kneel down behind a screen to protect himself from being hit, especially with less advanced hitters.

Drill #90: Open the Eyes and Hit

Objectives:
- Develops bat speed
- Improves reaction time
- Improves bat control
- Develops hand-eye coordination
- Improves balance

Degree of Difficulty:
- Soft toss: 3B
- Flips: 3B

Equipment Needed:
- Bat
- Baseballs
- Batting cage
- Hitting net
- Partner

Description: The hitter and the partner set themselves up in an underhand flip position. The hitter takes his normal stance and closes his eyes. When the partner lets go of the ball, he shouts "ball." The hitter then opens his eyes, finds the ball, and hits it right up the middle.

As the hitter gets better and quicker, the partner can wait a little longer to say "ball," making sure he still gives the hitter enough time to react to the ball.

Coaching Points:
- This should never be done during regular batting practice because it would be too dangerous.
- After finding the ball, the hitter needs to perform short, quick swings to the ball.
- This drill will not only help the hitter find the ball sooner, but also train him for the late movement of pitches such as sliders, cutters, and change-ups.
- The partner needs to move the ball around to make this drill a little more challenging.
- The partner should consider using a screen to protect himself.
- When first doing this drill, the partner needs to give the hitter extra time by saying "ball" before he lets go of it. As the hitter gets better he waits longer.
- If the hitter prefers, he can start this drill positioned as if he has already taken his stride.
- For younger hitters, a tee can be used. An adult can move the tee around, then yell ball. The adult needs to instruct the hitter to always wait for his command before he swings.
- The hitter can follow the 10 + 5 routine. He will quickly notice how big the ball looks when he is hitting the regular tosses.

Open eyes

BALL

8

Drills to Improve Hitting
Strength and Power

Drill #91: Resist-a-Bat

Objectives:
- Develops power
- Develops bat speed

Degree of Difficulty: 2B

Equipment Needed:
- Bat
- Partner
- Wall, pole, or tree

Description: This drill makes the hitter stronger by offering resistance in different locations on the swing path, thereby providing isometric resistance to the swing. It can be done two ways:

- A partner holds the barrel of the bat as the hitter is performing a slow motion swing. The partner gives the hitter resistance at different stages of the swing by holding the bat for a count or provides continuous resistance as the hitter goes through the swing. The hitter tries to overcome the resistance of the partner. The resistance should not be either too hard or too soft, so the hitter and his partner should experiment to find the right resistance level. Greater emphasis should be devoted to the area right before contact.

- If the hitter is by himself, he can utilize a sturdy, immovable object such as a wall. pole, or tree for the purpose of this drill. He lets that object provide the resistance while he moves himself around so he can work on different parts of his swing. The hitter will not be able to have continuous resistance throughout the swing when working on his own, but he will be able to pick a spot on his swing and hold for five to 10 seconds before moving to another location.

Coaching Points:
- This is a great drill for younger kids.
- The degree of difficulty varies depending on the amount of resistance used.
- The hitter needs to remember not to simply swing, but instead fight the resistance at particular points in the swing path.
- If necessary, the partner can use both of his hands in front of his chest to resist stronger hitters.
- This is a drill, not a game. The hitter must do anything foolish that could jeopardize the partner's safety.
- After every session the hitter should take a couple of swings for bat speed and swing feel.
- The hitter should not do this drill two days in a row and never right before a game.

Drill 92: Hitting a Deflated Basketball

Objectives:
- Develops power
- Develops bat speed
- Develops explosiveness and strengthens contact

Degree of Difficulty: 3B

Equipment Needed:
- Bat
- A deflated basketball, soccer ball, or volleyball
- Open space
- Optional: Baseballs, tee, plunger

Description: The hitter deflates an old basketball about half way. He needs to make sure that there is no bounce left in it. A partner tosses it to the hitter as an underhand flip from about 15 feet away or, if the hitter is by himself, he can set a plunger inside the tee hole to have it hold the basketball as the picture shows. The hitter takes his normal swing, putting total effort into each swing.

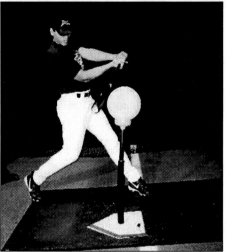

Coaching Points:
- This is another overload drill. It helps the hitter become stronger by hitting an object that is significantly heavier than a regular baseball. This drill also becomes a bat speed drill when the hitter hits a regular baseball after hitting the basketball. The difference in size gives the hitter a surprising amount of extra power.
- The most important thing about this drill is that the basketball not have any bounce left. If the ball bounces it can come back and hit the batter in the face.
- The hitter needs to try to stop his swing right after contact. This will focus his attention on the path of the swing where speed is most important.
- The hitter should try to follow the 10 + 5 routine, following every 10 swings with the basketball with five swings with some regular baseballs.

Drill #93: Hitting a Tire

Objectives:
- Improves power
- Improves bat speed

Degree of Difficulty: 2B

Equipment Needed:
- An old tire
- Rope
- Bat (preferably an old wooden one)

Description: A rope is tied around the tire (like a tire swing) and then it is hung from a tree or something similar. The tire should be around waist high, depending on what the hitter is working on (high, low pitches). The hitter hits the tire's tread, which will give in after being hit thus releasing all that tension and helping to avoid injury.

Coaching Points:
- The hitter can draw a baseball (with white paint) on each side of the tire's tread (low on one side, high on the other). This will incorporate hand-eye coordination into the drill.
- The hitter can take any kind of hitting practice right after each set of this drill. This will help develop bat speed.
- When the hitter hits a tire he is overloading his hitting muscles. Proper rest is essential; hitters should only perform this drill two or three times per week with at least a day off in between.
- A good program is three or four sets of 10 to 25 swings per session.
- To avoid injury, the hitter can tape his wrists or wear wristbands.

Drill #94: Swinging a Heavier Bat

Objectives:
- Develops power
- Improves bat speed
- Slows the swing down to allow for coaching tips

Degree of Difficulty:
- Dry swings: 1B
- Tee work: 1B
- Soft toss: 2B
- Flips: 2B
- Batting practice: 2B

Equipment Needed:
- A heavier bat
- A regular bat
- Baseballs
- Batting cage, net, or field

Description: The idea of this drill is to have the hitter swing a bat heavier than his regular bat, which will make the hitting muscles stronger and quicker. The hitter should use a bat about six to eight ounces heavier than his regular bat to accomplish this overload. The hitter can do this drill with the 10 + 5 approach, swinging 10 times with the heavier bat and five times with his normal bat.

Coaching Points:
- The degree of difficulty of this drill, regardless of how it is done, largely depends on the weight of the bat being used.
- To develop bat speed, a hitter needs to practice with different weight bats.
- The hitter needs to force himself to swing as fast as he does with his regular bat, as this is what develops bat speed.
- When picking a heavier bat, the hitter should choose one heavy enough to give him a good workout, but not so heavy that he cannot control it and use proper hitting mechanics.
- The hitter should do this drill during the off-season as much as possible.
- The hitter needs to have at least one day in between workouts and should not do it before a game because it will tire him out.

Drill #95: Heavy PVC Swings

Objectives:
• Improves arm strength
• Improves bat speed and power
• Smoothes the swing
• Improves hip flexibility
• Balances out both sides of the body (obliques)

Degree of Difficulty: 2B

Equipment Needed:
• PVC pipe (five feet long by $1\frac{1}{4}$ inches thick)
• Batting cage, baseball field, or open field

Description: Because the thickness and the length of the PVC pipe, it will feel relatively heavy in the hitters hands. To do this drill, the hitter stands as he normally does, pointing both feet toward the plate. He then takes a smooth swing, cutting through the air and trying to keep both feet and the hips pointing to the other side of the plate. The hitter listens to the sound of acceleration in the swing. The hitter should not try to pivot (i.e., turn the foot around); the swing and the extension of the arms will pull the back heel back. The hitter can visualize a rope connected from the hands to the back of the heel; the hands are pulling the heel around instead of allowing the heel to work

prematurely. After 10 swings, the hitter switches to the other side of the plate (i.e., switch-hits). He will feel how tight his normal front side is when he switch-hits, because all of the swings he takes the opposite way.

Coaching Points:
• This drill will not only increase front hip flexibility, but also balance the core area by working the weaker side of the midsection. This drill will also strengthen the hitter's hitting muscles, develop bat speed, and give the hitter feedback regarding the smoothness and extension of his swing (by the sound). Because the length and the heaviness of the pipe, the hitter has to finish the swing for him to avoid discomfort during the follow-through.
• Complement this drill with the power "V" PVC swings, in which the hitter holds the pipe about belly button–high and the pipe extends away from him parallel to the ground. The hitter then keeps the hands in the same place and takes the other end of the pipe to each shoulder, forming a "V." After a set of 10, the hitter reverses the position of the hands.
• The hitter should listen to the sound of the swing and should hear the acceleration of the swing out in front.
• The hitter needs to think "fast" (i.e., swing fast not hard).

Drill #96: Wrist Weight

Objectives:
- Develops power
- Develops bat speed
- Teaches how it feels to properly move the hands toward the ball

Degree of Difficulty:
- Dry swings: 2B
- Tee work: 2B
- Soft toss: 3B
- Flips: HR
- Batting practice: GS

Equipment Needed:
- A pair of wrist or ankle weights (1 to 5 lb.)
- Bat
- Baseballs
- Batting cage or net

Description: This is an overload (heavier than usual) and overspeed (faster than usual) drill. The hitter tightens the weights around his wrists, and then takes his natural swing. After he starts his swing he will notice how the hands just seem to go. When the hitter swings with the weights on, the swing will of course be slower. That's why it is best that he complete this drill by taking a few swings without them.

Coaching Points:
- Have the hitter perform a couple of sets of 10 repetitions with the weights on, followed by five swings without them.
- It is a good idea to progress from a lighter weight to a heavier one.
- The hitter should warm up correctly and make sure to rest between practice sessions.

Drill #97: Wrist Weight Five-Second Hold

Objectives:
- Improves arm strength
- Teaches the hitter to be more efficient during the swing
- Improves balance and core stability

Degree of Difficulty:
- Dry swings/tee work: 2B
- Soft toss/flips: 3B

Equipment Needed:
- Two ankle weights (size depends upon the hitter's age and strength)
- Bat
- Baseballs
- Batting cage
- Optional: Partner

Description: The hitter places a pair of ankle weights around his wrists and then takes his stride and his hands back. He then holds his hands back for five seconds. The partner tosses the ball and the hitter swings, trying to swing fast even though his hands feel heavy. The heavier the weight feels, the farther the hands go away from the body. When the weight feels light, the hitter has found his optimal launching position and beginning-of-swing approach.

Coaching Points:
- As mentioned earlier, the weight used should be determined by the hitter's strength, never going above five pounds. Young hitters should start with half-pound weights.
- Younger hitters can make their own wrist weights by filling a pair of sanitary socks (baseball socks) with sand.

Drill #98: The Power Pack

Objectives:
- Develops power
- Develops bat speed
- Improves endurance
- Develops explosiveness

Degree of Difficulty:
- Dry swings: 3B
- Tee work: 3B
- Soft toss: HR
- Flips: HR
- Batting practice GS

Equipment Needed:
- The hitter's regular bat
- A heavier bat
- A lighter bat
- Baseballs
- Batting cage, hitting net, baseball field, or open space
- Partner
- Optional: Tee

Description: The hitter needs three different size bats for this drill:

- A heavier bat—for overloading the hitting muscle. The hitter should use a bat approximately eight ounces heavier than his normal bat. If a heavier bat is not available, the hitter can use a heavy doughnut, a lightweight plate, a heavy pipe, a wood bat (if the hitter uses aluminum), or even an ankle weight tight around the bat.
- A lighter bat—for overspeeding the hitting muscles, making the hitter swing faster than usual. The hitter should use a bat about eight ounces lighter than his regular bat. If a lighter bat is not available, the hitter can use a broomstick, a PVC pipe, a plastic bat, or an aluminum bat (if the hitter hits with wood).
- His regular bat—for transferring the feeling he gets from using the other two bats to his regular swing.

The hitter starts by swinging the heavier bat 10 to 20 times, always trying to make each swing faster than the previous one. Then he uses the lighter bat and swings it 10 to 20 times, again trying to better himself with every swing. To finish the set, the hitter swings his normal bat 10 to 20 times. The hitter should compete against himself, always trying to swing faster and faster.

Coaching Points:
- A hitter can significantly improve his bat speed by following a swinging training program (similar to weight training).
- This is a very strenuous drill. As with weight training, rest is of great importance. The hitter can do this drill every other day. This should never be done before a game because of the fatigue factor. This a great drill for the off-season.
- The hitter should first do this drill with dry swings. After mastering it, he can involve a ball in this drill.

Drill #99: Hitting with a Wood Bat

Objectives:
- Develops power
- Improves hitting mechanics
- Gives the hitter instant feedback regarding how he has hit the ball
- Develops bat speed (if combined with an aluminum bat)
- Improves bat control

Degree of Difficulty:
- Dry swings/tee work: 1B
- Soft toss/flips: 2B
- Batting practice: 3B

Equipment Needed:
- Wood bat
- Baseballs
- Batting cage, hitting net, baseball field, or open space
- Partner
- Optional: Aluminum bat, tee

Description: This is an easy drill to perform, but a difficult one to do well. The hitter simply takes a wood bat and hits with it.

Coaching Points:
- A wood bat is probably the best hitting device on the market. It really teaches a hitter how to hit. If the hitter does follow proper mechanics he will receive immediate feedback, by the way the bat felt in his hands, the nature of the hit, or by the fact that the bat broke. If the hitter is dreaming of one day playing professional baseball, he should start using a wood bat as soon as possible so he gets used to it.

- If the hitter does not hit the ball where he is supposed to (i.e., on the sweet spot), he will know it. Using an aluminum bat might give the hitter the wrong idea about what kind of hitter he is. Many hitters do not get drafted because scouts feel that they only have "aluminum bat power" and that they will not be able to transfer that power to a wood bat.

- With an aluminum bat the hitter does not need to hit the ball on the sweet spot to hit the ball pretty hard. In addition, aluminum bats do not break as often, so hitters are not afraid to get "jammed" and pitchers do not like to throw inside because they are scared the ball will hit out of the park. Because the bat is so much lighter, it helps the hitter produce more bat speed than he truly possesses.

- Using a wooden bat makes the hitter stronger. The fact that the balance point is closer to the barrel makes the bat feel heavier than an aluminum bat of the same weight. Because the bat is heavier, the batter's hitting muscles will get stronger over time. And when he goes back to his aluminum bat, he will hit the ball even harder. It also makes the hitter's hands tougher.

- To ease the sizable investment of purchasing a wood bat, tell players to only use their wood bat during batting practice.

- When a wood bat breaks, the player may sometimes be able to nail it back together for use in batting practice. He can also nail a strip of rubber from an old bicycle tube stretched over the break, adding a little more life to the bat.

- Taping the barrel at the sweet spot will buy a hitter some time also. It helps protect the bat from splintering too soon.

Drill #100: Self-Serve Power

Objectives:
- Develops power
- Improves arm extension on contact
- Improves bat control
- Develops hand-eye coordination
- Improves use of the legs during the swing

Degree of Difficulty: 2B

Equipment Needed:
- Bat
- Baseballs
- Baseball field or open space

Description: The hitter stands at home plate and proceeds to perform "power fungo." The hitter holds a ball with one hand and a bat with his other. The hitter then tosses the ball to himself and tries to hit the ball out of the park on a line drive. The hitter provides all the power (as opposed to the power generated by a pitched ball), so by putting everything into the swing he will get stronger.

Coaching Points:
- The hitter needs to use all parts of the field to challenge himself and avoid grooving his swing to one location.
- The hitter should not get discouraged if he does not hit the ball out of the park. Instead, the hitter needs to try to better himself each time he does this drill. He should compete against himself or a friend to make it more fun.
- If any players are on the field, the hitter needs to let them know what he is doing so they pay attention and do not get hit by the ball.

Drill #101: Turning the Hitter

Objectives:
- Increases hip flexibility
- Improves rotation

Degree of Difficulty: 1B

Equipment Needed:
- Partner
- Bat
- Open space

Description: The hitter goes to his regular follow-through with the partner standing behind him. The partner then puts one hand behind the back shoulder and the other hand in front of the front shoulder. With the hitter trying to look at the plate while not moving any body parts, the partner turns the hitter even more and holds for a count of five. The partner then lets him go back to his regular launching position and repeats the drill four more times. The hitter then takes some swings while trying to keep his head down and get all the way to where the partner turned him.

Coaching Point:
- This drill can be done before every game or batting practice. It not only makes the hitter more flexible, but also helps him become more powerful.

About the Author

Luis Ortiz has 14 years of professional baseball experience, including playing in the Majors with the Red Sox and the Texas Rangers. For most of his minor league career, he maintained a batting average over .300.

After growing up playing baseball in the Dominican Republic, Luis earned a baseball scholarship from Union University in Jackson, TN, where he set many of Union's batting average and home run records, as well as the NAIA career slugging percentage record. In 1991, Luis was drafted in the eighth round by the Boston Red Sox.

Thirteen years after his first college stint, Luis went back to school and graduated with a bachelor's degree in physical education. Luis has been offered numerous coaching positions with professional organizations. He has opened the Athletic Village Baseball and Softball School, a state-of-the-art instructional baseball school in Keller, Texas, in the Dallas-Fort Worth area.

His book *The Natural Hitter's Handbook* is also available from Coaches Choice.